THE ZEN TEACHING *of*

Bodhidharma

Translated and with an Introduction by Red Pine

MACMILLAN

This edition published in India 2019 by Macmillan
an imprint of Pan Macmillan Publishing India,
Pan Macmillan India, 707, Kailash Building
26, K. G. Marg, New Delhi – 110 001
www.panmacmillan.co.in

Pan Macmillan, The Smithson, 6 Briset Street, London EC1M 5NR,
Basingstoke and Oxford
Associated companies throughout the world
www.panmacmillan.com

ISBN 978-93-86215-87-1

7

Printed and bound in India by Thomson Press India Private Limited

FSC
www.fsc.org
MIX
Paper | Supporting responsible forestry
FSC® C010615

for John Blofeld

CONTENTS

INTRODUCTION

Buddhism came to China 2,000 years ago. As early as A.D. 65, a community of Buddhist monks was reported living under royal patronage in the northern part of Kiangsu Province, not far from the birthplace of Confucius, and the first monks had probably arrived a hundred years earlier. Since then, tens of thousands of Indian and Central Asian monks have journeyed to China by land and sea, but among those who brought the teachings of the Buddha to China, none has had an impact comparable to that of Bodhidharma.

Unknown to all but a few disciples during his lifetime, Bodhidharma is the patriarch of millions of Zen Buddhists and students of kung-fu. He is the subject of many legends as well. Along with zen and kung-fu, Bodhidharma reportedly also brought tea to China. To keep from falling asleep while meditating, he cut off his eyelids, and where they fell, tea bushes grew. Since then, tea has become the beverage of not only monks but everyone in the Orient. Faithful to this tradition, artists invariably depict Bodhidharma with bulging, lidless eyes.

As often happens with legends, it's become impossible to separate fact from fiction. His dates are uncertain; in fact, I know at least one Buddhist scholar who doubts that Bodhidharma ever existed. But at the risk of writing about a man who never lived, I've sketched a likely biography, based on the earliest records and a few of my own surmises, to provide a backdrop for the sermons attributed to him.

Bodhidharma was born around the year 440 in Kanchi, the capital of the Southern Indian kingdom of Pallava. He was a Brahman by birth and the third son of King Simhavarman. When he was young, he was converted to Buddhism, and later he received instruction in the Dharma from Prajnatara, whom his father had invited from the ancient Buddhist heartland of Magadha. It was Prajnatara who also told Bodhidharma to go to China. Since the traditional overland route was blocked by the Huns, and since Pallava had commercial ties throughout Southeast Asia, Bodhidharma left by ship from the nearby port of Mahaballipuram. After skirting the Indian coast and the Malay Peninsula for three years, he finally arrived in Southern China around 475.

At that time the country was divided into the Northern Wei and Liu Sung dynasties. This division of China into a series of northern and southern dynasties had begun in the early third century and continued until the country was reunited under the Sui dynasty in the late sixth century. It was during this period of division and strife that Indian Buddhism developed into Chinese Buddhism, with the more military-minded northerners emphasizing meditation and magic and the more intellectual southerners preferring philosophical discussion and the intuitive grasp of principles.

When Bodhidharma arrived in China, in the latter part of the fifth century, there were approximately 2,000 Buddhist temples and 36,000 clergy in the South. In the North, a census in 477 counted 6,500 temples and nearly 80,000 clergy. Less than fifty years later, another census conducted in the North raised these figures to 30,000 temples and 2,000,000 clergy, or about 5 percent of the population. This undoubtedly included many people who were trying to avoid taxes and conscription or who sought the protection of the Church for other, nonreligious, reasons, but clearly Buddhism was spreading among the common people north of the Yangtze. In the South, it remained largely confined to the educated elite until well into the sixth century.

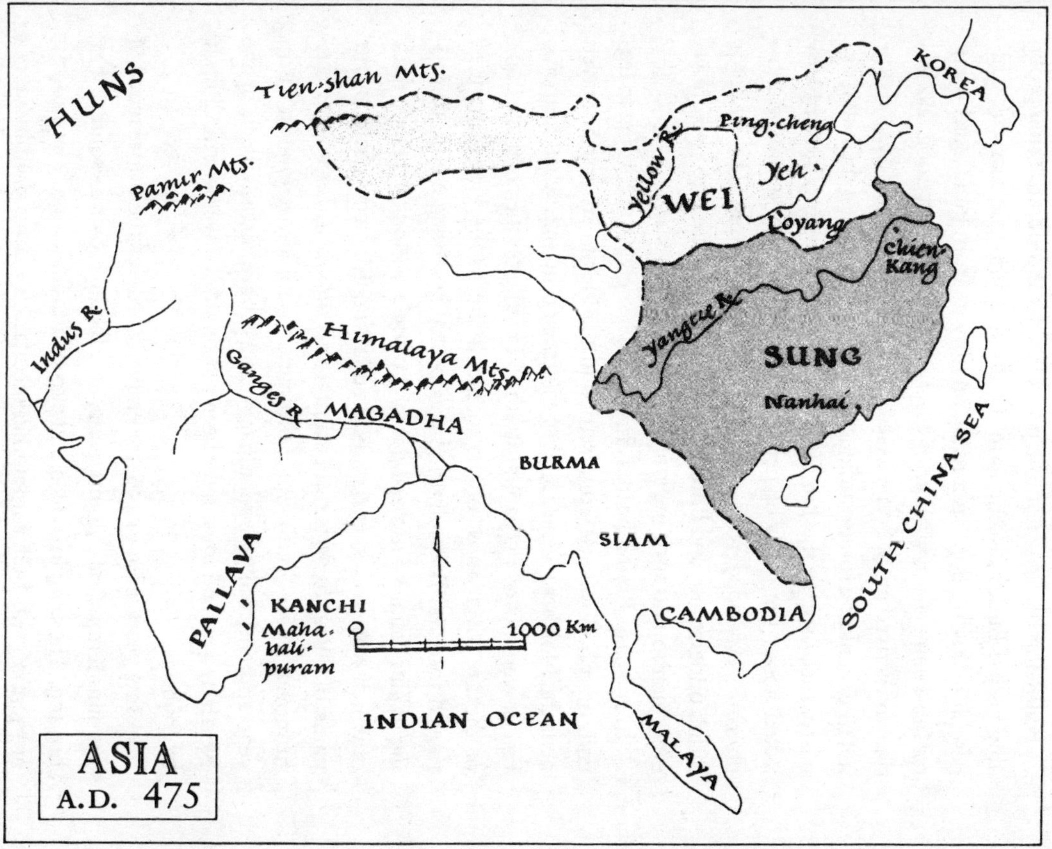
HUNS
Tien-shan Mts.
Pamir Mts.
KOREA
Ping-cheng
Yeh
Yellow R.
WEI
Loyang
Chien-Kang
Yangtze R.
SUNG
Nanhai
Indus R.
Himalaya Mts.
Ganges R.
MAGADHA
BURMA
SIAM
SOUTH CHINA SEA
PALLAVA
KANCHI
Maha-bali-puram
1000 Km
CAMBODIA
INDIAN OCEAN
MALAYA
ASIA
A.D. 475

Following his arrival in the port of Nanhai, Bodhidharma probably visited Buddhist centers in the South and began learning Chinese, if he hadn't done so already on his way from India. According to Tao-yuan's *Transmission of the Lamp*, finished in 1002, Bodhidharma arrived in the South as late as 520 and was invited to the capital in Chienkang for an audience with Emperor Wu of the Liang dynasty, successor to the Liu Sung. During this meeting the emperor asked about the merit of performing religious works, and Bodhidharma responded with the doctrine of emptiness. The emperor didn't understand, and Bodhidharma left. The earliest records, however, mention no such meeting.

In any case, Bodhidharma crossed the Yangtze—according to legend, on a hollow reed—and settled in the North. At first he stayed near the Northern Wei capital of Pingcheng. In 494, when Emperor Hsiao-wen moved his capital south to Loyang on the northern bank of the Lo River, most of the monks living in the Pingcheng area moved too, and Bodhidharma was probably among them. According to Tao-hsuan's *Further Lives of Exemplary Monks*, the first draft of which was written in 645, Bodhidharma ordained a monk by the name of Sheng-fu. When the capital was moved to Loyang, Sheng-fu moved to the South. Since ordination normally requires a three-year apprenticeship, Bodhidharma must have already been in the North by 490 and must have been reasonably conversant in Chinese by then.

A few years later, in 496, the emperor ordered the construction of Shaolin Temple on Mount Sung, in Honan Province southeast of Loyang. The temple, which still exists (although largely as a tourist attraction), was built for another meditation master from India, not for Bodhidharma. But while zen masters have come and gone at the temple for the past 1,500 years, Bodhidharma is the only monk anyone but a Buddhist historian associates with Shaolin. It was here, on Mount Sung's western Shaoshih Peak, that Bodhidharma is said to have spent nine years in meditation, facing the rock wall of a cave about a mile from the temple. Shaolin later became famous for training monks in kung-fu, and Bodhidharma is honored as the founder of this art as well. Coming from India, he undoubtedly instructed his disciples in some form of yoga, but no early records mention him teaching any exercise or martial art.

By the year 500, Loyang was one of the largest cities in the world, with a population of over half a million. When Emperor Hsuan-wu died in 516 and the Empress Dowager Ling assumed control of the government, one of her first acts was to order the construction of Yung-ning Temple. The construction of this temple and its 400-foot-high pagoda nearly exhausted the imperial treasury. According to a record of Loyang's temples written in 547 by Yang Hsuan-chih, the golden wind-chimes that hung along the temple's eaves could be heard for three miles and the spire of the temple's pagoda could be seen over thirty miles away. Yang's account includes the comments of a monk from the West named Bodhidharma, who called it the most imposing structure he had ever seen. Since the temple wasn't built until 516 and was destroyed by fire in 534, Bodhidharma must have been in the capital around 520. Early records say he traveled throughout the Loyang area, coming and going with the seasons. In the capital, though, he must have stayed at Yung-ming Temple. Not to be confused with Yung-ning Temple, Yung-ming had been built a few years earlier, at the beginning of the sixth century, by Emperor Hsuan-wu as a headquarters for foreign monks. Before the mass evacuation of the city during the collapse of the Northern Wei in 534, the temple reportedly housed over 3,000 monks from countries as far away as Syria.

Despite the sudden popularity of Buddhism in China, Bodhidharma found few disciples. Besides Sheng-fu, who moved to the South soon after his ordination, the only other disciples mentioned are Tao-yu and Hui-k'o, both of whom are said to have studied with Bodhidharma for five to six years. Tao-yu, we're told, understood the Way but never taught. It was to Hui-k'o that Bodhidharma entrusted the robe and bowl of his lineage and, according to Tao-hsuan, a copy of Gunabhadra's translation of the *Lankavatara Sutra*. In the sermons translated here, though, Bodhidharma quotes mostly from the *Nirvana*, *Avatamsaka*, and *Vimilakirti* sutras and uses none of the terminology characteristic of the *Lankavatara*. Perhaps it was Hui-k'o, not Bodhidharma, who thought so highly of this sutra.

In his *Transmission of the Lamp*, Tao-yuan says that soon after he had transmitted the patriarchship of his lineage to Hui-k'o, Bodhidharma died in 528 on the fifth day of the tenth month, poisoned by a jealous monk. Tao-hsuan's much earlier biography of Bodhidharma says only that he died on the banks of the Lo River and doesn't mention the date or cause of death. According to Tao-yuan, Bodhidharma's remains were interred near Loyang at Tinglin Temple on Bear Ear Mountain. Tao-yuan adds that three years later an official met Bodhidharma walking in the mountains of Central Asia. He was carrying a staff from which hung a single sandal, and he told the official he was going back to India. Reports of this meeting aroused the curiosity of other monks, who finally agreed to open Bodhidharma's tomb. But inside all they found was a single sandal, and ever since then Bodhidharma has been pictured carrying a staff from which hangs the missing sandal.

With the assassination of Emperor Hsiao-wu in 534, the Northern Wei split into the Western and Eastern Wei dynasties, and Loyang came under attack. Since the powerful Kao family of the Eastern Wei was renowned for its patronage of Buddhism, many of the monks living in Loyang, including Hui-k'o, moved to the Eastern Wei capital of Yeh. There Hui-k'o eventually met T'an-lin. T'an-lin worked first in Loyang and later in Yeh writing prefaces and commentaries to new translations of Buddhist sutras. After meeting Hui-k'o, he became interested in Bodhidharma's approach to Buddhism and added a brief preface to the *Outline of Practice*. In this preface he says that Bodhidharma came from Southern India and that following his arrival in China, he found only two worthy disciples, Hui-k'o and Tao-yu. He also says that Bodhidharma taught wall meditation and the four practices described in the *Outline*.

If this is all we know about Bodhidharma, why, then, is he the most famous of all the millions of monks who have studied and taught the Dharma in China? The reason is that he alone is credited with bringing zen to China. Of course, zen, as meditation, had been taught and practiced for several hundred years before Bodhidharma arrived. And much of what he had to say concerning doctrine had been said before—by Tao-sheng, for example, a hundred years earlier. But Bodhidharma's approach to zen was unique. As he says in these sermons, "Seeing your nature is zen. . . . Not thinking about anything is zen. . . . Everything you do is zen." While others viewed zen as purification of the mind or as a stage on the way to buddhahood, Bodhidharma equated zen with buddhahood—and buddhahood with the mind, the everyday mind. Instead of telling his disciples to purify their minds, he pointed them to rock walls, to the movements of tigers and cranes, to a hollow reed floating across the Yangtze, to a single sandal. Bodhidharma's zen was Mahayana Zen, not Hinayana Zen—the sword of wisdom, not the meditation cushion. As did other masters, he undoubtedly instructed his disciples in Buddhist discipline, meditation, and doctrine, but he used the sword that Prajnatara had given him to cut their minds free from rules, trances, and scriptures. Such a sword, though, is hard to grasp and hard to use. Small wonder that his sole successor, Hui-k'o, was a one-armed man.

But such a radical understanding of zen didn't originate with Bodhidharma or with Prajnatara. It's said that one day Brahma, lord of creation, offered the Buddha a flower and asked him to preach the Dharma. When the Buddha held up the flower, his audience was puzzled, except for Kashyapa, who smiled. This is how zen began. And this is how it was transmitted: with a flower, with a rock wall, with a shout. This approach, once it was made known by Bodhidharma and his successors, revolutionized the understanding and practice of Buddhism in China.

Such an approach doesn't come across very well in books. But in his *Further Lives of Exemplary Monks*, Tao-hsuan says that Bodhidharma's teachings were written down. Most scholars agree that the *Outline of Practice* is one such record, but opinion is divided concerning the other three sermons translated here. All three have long been attributed to Bodhidharma, but in recent years a number of scholars have suggested that these sermons are the work of later disciples. Yanagida, for example, attributes the *Bloodstream Sermon* to a member of the Oxhead Zen School, which flourished in the seventh and eighth centuries, and he thinks that the *Wake-up Sermon* was an eighth-century work of the Northern Zen School and the *Breakthrough Sermon* was by Shen-hsiu, the seventh-century patriarch of the Northern Zen School.

Unfortunately, evidence that would conclusively prove or disprove the traditional attribution is lacking. Until the present century, the earliest known copies of these sermons were fourteenth-century versions of T'ang dynasty (618–907) originals in the collection of

Japan's Kanazawa Bunko. But with the discovery of thousands of T'ang dynasty Buddhist manuscripts earlier this century in China's Tunhuang Caves, we now have seventh- and eighth-century copies. Clearly these sermons were compiled at a very early date by monks who traced their ancestry to Bodhidharma. If it wasn't Hui-k'o or one of his disciples, perhaps it was T'an-lin who wrote them down. In any case, in the absence of convincing evidence to the contrary, I see no reason why they shouldn't be accepted as the sermons of the man to whom they've been attributed for more than 1,200 years.

Bodhidharma's disciples were few, and the Zen tradition that traced its ancestry to him didn't begin its full flowering until nearly two hundred years after his death. Given the spontaneity and detachment fostered by Bodhidharma's approach to zen, it's easy to see why these sermons were eventually neglected in favor of those by native Chinese zen masters. By comparison Bodhidharma's sermons seem somewhat alien and bare. I only found them myself by accident, in an edition of Huang-po's *Essentials on the Transmission of Mind*. That was twelve years ago. Since then I've grown quite fond of their bare-bones zen, and I've often wondered why they aren't more popular. But popular or not, here they are again. Before they fade once more into the dust of some crypt or library, read them through once or twice and look for the one thing that Bodhidharma brought to China: look for the print of the mind.

Red Pine
Bamboo Lake, Taiwan
Big Cold, Year of the Tiger

THE ZEN TEACHING *of*

Bodhidharma

菩提達磨大師略辨大乘入道四行觀

夫入道多途。要而言之。不出二種。一是理入。二是行入。理入者。謂藉教悟宗。深信含生同一眞性。但爲客塵妄想所覆。不能顯了。若也捨妄歸眞。凝住壁觀。無自無他。凡聖等一。堅住不移。更不隨文教。此卽與理冥符。無有分別。寂然無爲。名之理入。行入謂四行。其餘諸行悉入此中。何等四耶。一報冤行。二隨緣行。三無所求行。四稱法行。云何

報冤行。謂修道行人。若受苦時。當自念言。我往昔無數劫中。棄本從末。流浪諸有。多起冤憎。違害無限。今雖無

Outline of Practice

MANY roads lead to the Path,[1] but basically there are only two: reason and practice. To enter by reason means to realize the essence through instruction and to believe that all living things share the same true nature, which isn't apparent because it's shrouded by sensation and delusion. Those who turn from delusion back to reality, who meditate on walls,[2] the absence of self and other, the oneness of mortal and sage, and who remain unmoved even by scriptures are in complete and unspoken agreement with reason. Without moving, without effort, they enter, we say, by reason.

To enter by practice refers to four all-inclusive practices:[3] suffering injustice, adapting to conditions, seeking nothing, and practicing the Dharma.

First, suffering injustice. When those who search for the Path encounter adversity, they should think to themselves, "In countless ages gone by, I've turned from the essential to the trivial and wandered through all manner of existence, often angry without cause and guilty of numberless transgressions. Now, though I do no wrong, I'm punished by my past. Neither gods nor men can

犯。是我宿殃。惡業果熟。非天非人所能見與。甘心甘受
都無寃訴。經云。逢苦不憂。何以故。識達故。此心生時。與
理相應。體寃進道。故說言報寃行。
二隨緣行者。衆生無我。並緣業所轉。苦樂齊受。皆從緣
生。若得勝報榮譽等事。是我過去宿因所感。今方得之。
緣盡還無。何喜之有。得失從緣。心無增減。喜風不動。冥
順於道。是故說言隨緣行。
三無所求行者。世人長迷。處處貪著。名之爲求。智者悟
眞。理將俗反。安心無爲。形隨運轉。萬有斯空。無所願樂。
功德黑暗。常相隨逐。三界久居。猶如火宅。有身皆苦。誰
得而安。了達此處。故捨諸有。止想無求。經曰。有求皆苦。

foresee when an evil deed will bear its fruit. I accept it with an open heart and without complaint of injustice." The sutras say, "When you meet with adversity don't be upset, because it makes sense." With such understanding you're in harmony with reason. And by suffering injustice you enter the Path.

Second, adapting to conditions. As mortals, we're ruled by conditions, not by ourselves. All the suffering and joy we experience depend on conditions. If we should be blessed by some great reward, such as fame or fortune, it's the fruit of a seed planted by us in the past. When conditions change, it ends. Why delight in its existence? But while success and failure depend on conditions, the mind neither waxes nor wanes. Those who remain unmoved by the wind of joy silently follow the Path.

Third, seeking nothing. People of this world are deluded. They're always longing for something—always, in a word, seeking. But the wise wake up. They choose reason over custom. They fix their minds on the sublime and let their bodies change with the seasons. All phenomena are empty. They contain nothing worth desiring. Calamity forever alternates with Prosperity.[4] To dwell in the three realms[5] is to dwell in a burning house. To have a body is to suffer. Does anyone with a body know peace? Those who understand this detach themselves from all that exists and stop imagining or seeking anything. The sutras say, "To seek is to suffer.

無求卽樂判知無求眞爲道行故言無所求行。

四稱法行者性淨之理目之爲法此理衆相斯空無染無著無此無彼經曰法無衆生離衆生垢故法無有我離我垢故智者若能信解此理應當稱法而行法體無慳身命財行檀捨施心無悋惜脫解三空不倚不著但爲去垢稱化衆生而不取相此爲自行復能利他亦能莊嚴菩提之道檀施既爾餘五亦然爲除妄想修行六度而無所行是爲稱法行。

達磨大師四行觀終

To seek nothing is bliss." When you seek nothing, you're on the Path.

Fourth, practicing the Dharma.[6] The Dharma is the truth that all natures are pure. By this truth, all appearances are empty. Defilement and attachment, subject and object don't exist. The sutras say, "The Dharma includes no being because it's free from the impurity of being, and the Dharma includes no self because it's free from the impurity of self." Those wise enough to believe and understand this truth are bound to practice according to the Dharma. And since that which is real includes nothing worth begrudging, they give their body, life, and property in charity, without regret, without the vanity of giver, gift, or recipient, and without bias or attachment. And to eliminate impurity they teach others, but without becoming attached to form. Thus, through their own practice they're able to help others and glorify the Way of Enlightenment. And as with charity, they also practice the other virtues. But while practicing the six virtues[7] to eliminate delusion, they practice nothing at all. This is what's meant by practicing the Dharma.

達磨大師血脉論

三界混起。同歸一心。前佛後佛。以心傳心。不立文字。問曰。若不立文字。以何爲心。答曰。汝問吾。卽是汝心。吾答汝。卽是吾心。吾若無心。因何解答汝。汝若無心。因何解問吾。問吾卽是汝心。從無始曠大劫以來。乃至施爲運動。一切時中。一切處所。皆是汝本心。皆是汝本佛。卽心是佛。亦復如是。除此心外。終無別佛可得。離此心外。覓菩提涅槃。無有是處。自性眞實。非因非果。法卽是心義。自心是涅槃。若言心外有佛及菩提可得。無有是處。佛及菩提皆在何處。譬如有人以手捉虛空得否。虛空但

Bloodstream Sermon

Everything that appears in the three realms comes from the mind.[8] Hence buddhas[9] of the past and future teach mind to mind without bothering about definitions.[10]

But if they don't define it, what do they mean by mind?

You ask. That's your mind. I answer. That's my mind. If I had no mind, how could I answer? If you had no mind, how could you ask? That which asks is your mind. Through endless kalpas[11] without beginning, whatever you do, wherever you are, that's your real mind, that's your real buddha. *This mind is the buddha*[12] says the same thing. Beyond this mind you'll never find another buddha. To search for enlightenment[13] or nirvana[14] beyond this mind is impossible. The reality of your own self-nature,[15] the absence of cause and effect, is what's meant by mind. Your mind is nirvana. You might think you can find a buddha or enlightenment somewhere beyond the mind, but such a place doesn't exist.

Trying to find a buddha or enlightenment is like trying to grab space. Space has a name but no form. It's not something you

有名。亦無相貌。取不得。捨不得。是捉空不得。除此心外見佛。終不得也。佛是自心作得。因何離此心外覓佛。前佛後佛只言其心。心卽是佛。佛卽是心。心外無佛。佛外無心。若言心外有佛。佛在何處。心外旣無佛。何起佛見。遞相誑惑。不能了本心。被它無情物攝。無自由。若也不信。自誑無益。佛無過患。衆生顚倒。不覺不知自心是佛。若知自心是佛。不應心外覓佛。佛不度佛。將心覓佛。不識佛。但是外覓佛者。盡是不識自心是佛。亦不得將佛禮佛。不得將心念佛。佛不誦經。佛不持戒。佛不犯戒。佛無持犯。亦不造善惡。若欲覓佛。須是見性。見性卽是佛。若不見性。念佛誦經持齋持戒亦無益處。念佛得因果。

can pick up or put down. And you certainly can't grab it. Beyond this mind you'll never see a buddha. The buddha is a product of your mind. Why look for a buddha beyond this mind?

Buddhas of the past and future only talk about this mind. The mind is the buddha, and the buddha is the mind. Beyond the mind there's no buddha, and beyond the buddha there's no mind. If you think there's a buddha beyond the mind, where is he? There's no buddha beyond the mind, so why envision one? You can't know your real mind as long as you deceive yourself. As long as you're enthralled by a lifeless form, you're not free. If you don't believe me, deceiving yourself won't help. It's not the buddha's fault. People, though, are deluded. They're unaware that their own mind is the buddha. Otherwise they wouldn't look for a buddha outside the mind.

Buddhas don't save buddhas. If you use your mind to look for a buddha, you won't see the buddha. As long as you look for a buddha somewhere else, you'll never see that your own mind is the buddha. Don't use a buddha to worship a buddha. And don't use the mind to invoke a buddha.[16] Buddhas don't recite sutras.[17] Buddhas don't keep precepts.[18] And buddhas don't break precepts. Buddhas don't keep or break anything. Buddhas don't do good or evil.

To find a buddha, you have to see your nature.[19] Whoever sees his nature is a buddha. If you don't see your nature, invoking buddhas, reciting sutras, making offerings, and keeping precepts are all useless. Invoking buddhas results in good karma, reciting sutras results in a good memory; keeping precepts results in a

誦經得聰明。持戒得生天。布施得福報。覓佛終不得也。若自己不明了。須參善知識。了卻生死根本。若不見性。卽不名善知識。若不如此縱說得十二部經亦不免生死輪迴。三界受苦。無出期。時昔有善星比丘。誦得十二部經猶自不免輪迴。緣爲不見性。善星旣如此。今時人講得三五本經論以爲佛法者。愚人也。若不識得自心。誦得閑文書。都無用處。若要覓佛。直須見性。性卽是佛。佛卽是自在人。無事無作人。若不見性。終日茫茫。向外馳求。覓佛元來不得。雖無一物可得。若求會。亦須參善知識。切須苦求。令心會解。生死事大。不得空過。自誑無益。縱有珍珤如山。眷屬如恒河沙。開眼卽見。合眼還見

good rebirth, and making offerings results in future blessings—but no buddha.

If you don't understand by yourself, you'll have to find a teacher to get to the bottom of life and death.[20] But unless he sees his nature, such a person isn't a teacher. Even if he can recite the Twelvefold Canon,[21] he can't escape the Wheel of Birth and Death.[22] He suffers in the three realms without hope of release.

Long ago, the monk Good Star[23] was able to recite the entire Canon. But he didn't escape the Wheel, because he didn't see his nature. If this was the case with Good Star, then people nowadays who recite a few sutras or shastras[24] and think it's the Dharma are fools. Unless you see your mind, reciting so much prose is useless.

To find a buddha all you have to do is see your nature. Your nature is the buddha. And the buddha is the person who's free: free of plans, free of cares. If you don't see your nature and run around all day looking somewhere else, you'll never find a buddha. The truth is, there's nothing to find. But to reach such an understanding you need a teacher and you need to struggle to make yourself understand. Life and death are important. Don't suffer them in vain. There's no advantage in deceiving yourself. Even if you have mountains of jewels and as many servants as there are grains of sand along the Ganges, you see them when your eyes are open. But

麽。故知有爲之法。如夢幻等。若不急尋師。空過一生。然卽佛性自有。若不因師。終不明了。不因師悟者。萬中希有。若自己以緣會合。得聖人意。卽不用參善知識。此卽是生而知之。勝學也。若未悟解。須勤苦參學。因教方得悟。若未悟了。不學亦得。不異迷人。不能分別皂白。妄言宣佛勑。謗佛忌法。如斯等類。說法如雨。盡是魔說。卽非佛說。師是魔王。弟子是魔民。迷人任它指揮。不覺墮生死海。但是不見性人。妄稱是佛。此等衆生。是大罪人。誑它一切衆生。令入魔界。若不見性。說得十二部經教。盡是魔說。魔家眷屬。不是佛家弟子。旣不辨皂白。憑何免生死。若見性卽是佛。不見性卽是衆生。若離衆生性。別

what about when your eyes are shut? You should realize then that everything you see is like a dream or illusion.

If you don't find a teacher soon, you'll live this life in vain. It's true, you have the buddha-nature. But without the help of a teacher you'll never know it. Only one person in a million becomes enlightened without a teacher's help.

If, though, by the conjunction of conditions, someone understands what the Buddha meant, that person doesn't need a teacher. Such a person has a natural awareness superior to anything taught. But unless you're so blessed, study hard, and by means of instruction you'll understand.

People who don't understand and think they can do so without study are no different from those deluded souls who can't tell white from black.[25] Falsely proclaiming the Buddhadharma, such persons in fact blaspheme the Buddha and subvert the Dharma. They preach as if they were bringing rain. But theirs is the preaching of devils,[26] not of buddhas. Their teacher is the King of Devils and their disciples are the Devil's minions. Deluded people who follow such instruction unwittingly sink deeper in the Sea of Birth and Death.

Unless they see their nature, how can people call themselves buddhas? They're liars who deceive others into entering the realm of devils. Unless they see their nature, their preaching of the Twelvefold Canon is nothing but the preaching of devils. Their allegiance is to Mara, not to the Buddha. Unable to distinguish white from black, how can they escape birth and death?

Whoever sees his nature is a buddha; whoever doesn't is a mortal. But if you can find your buddha-nature apart from your

有佛性可得者。佛今在何處。即衆生性。即是佛性也。性外無佛。佛即是性。除此性外。無佛可得。佛外無性可得。問曰。若不見性。念佛誦經布施持戒精進。廣興福利。得成佛否。答曰。不得。又問。因何不得。答曰。有少法可得。是有爲法。是因果。是受報。是輪迴法。不免生死。何時得成佛道。成佛須是見性。若不見性。因果等語。是外道法。若是佛。不習外道法。佛是無業人。無因果。但有少法可得。盡是謗佛。憑何得成。但有住著一心一能一解一見。佛都不許。佛無持犯。心性本空。亦非垢淨。諸法無修無證。無因無果。佛不持戒。佛不修善。佛不造惡。佛不精進。佛不懈怠。佛是無作人。但有住著心。見佛即不許也。佛不

mortal nature, where is it? Our mortal nature is our buddha-nature. Beyond this nature there's no buddha. The buddha is our nature. There's no buddha besides this nature. And there's no nature besides the buddha.

But suppose I don't see my nature, can't I still attain enlightenment by invoking buddhas, reciting sutras, making offerings, observing precepts, practicing devotions, or doing good works?

No, you can't.

Why not?

If you attain anything at all, it's conditional, it's karmic. It results in retribution. It turns the Wheel. And as long as you're subject to birth and death, you'll never attain enlightenment. To attain enlightenment you have to see your nature. Unless you see your nature, all this talk about cause and effect is nonsense. Buddhas don't practice nonsense. A buddha is free of karma,[27] free of cause and effect. To say he attains anything at all is to slander a buddha. What could he possibly attain? Even focusing on a mind, a power, an understanding, or a view is impossible for a buddha. A buddha isn't one-sided. The nature of his mind is basically empty, neither pure nor impure. He's free of practice and realization. He's free of cause and effect.

A buddha doesn't observe precepts. A buddha doesn't do good or evil. A buddha isn't energetic or lazy. A buddha is someone who does nothing, someone who can't even focus his mind on a buddha. A buddha isn't a buddha. Don't think about buddhas. If

是佛。莫作佛解。若不見此義。一切時中。一切處處。皆是不了本心。若不見性。一切時中擬作無作想。是大罪人。是癡人。落無記空中。昏昏如醉人。不辨好惡。若擬修無作法。先須見性。然後息緣慮。若不見性得成佛道。無有是處。有人撥無因果。熾然作惡業。妄言本空。作惡無過。如此之人。墮無間黑暗地獄。永無出期。若是智人。不應作如是見解。

問曰。既若施為運動。一切時中皆是本心。色身無常之時。云何不見本心。答曰。本心常現前。汝自不見。

問曰。心既見在。何故不見。師曰。汝曾作夢否。答曾作夢。

問曰。汝作夢之時是汝本身否。答是本身。 又問。汝言

you don't see what I'm talking about, you'll never know your own mind.

People who don't see their nature and imagine they can practice thoughtlessness all the time are liars and fools. They fall into endless space. They're like drunks. They can't tell good from evil. If you intend to cultivate such a practice, you have to see your nature before you can put an end to rational thought. To attain enlightenment without seeing your nature is impossible.

Still others commit all sorts of evil deeds, claiming karma doesn't exist. They erroneously maintain that since everything is empty, committing evil isn't wrong. Such persons fall into a hell of endless darkness with no hope of release. Those who are wise hold no such conception.

But if our every movement or state, whenever it occurs, is the mind, why don't we see this mind when a person's body dies?

The mind is always present. You just don't see it.

But if the mind is present, why don't I see it?

Do you ever dream?

Of course.

When you dream, is that you?

Yes, it's me.

語施爲運動與汝別不別。答曰。不別。 師曰。旣若不別。
卽此身是汝本法身。卽此法身是汝本心。此心從無始
曠大劫來與如今不別。未曾有生死。不生不滅。不增不
減。不垢不淨。不好不惡。不來不去。亦無是非。亦無男女
相。亦無僧俗老少。無聖無凡。亦無佛。亦無衆生。亦無修
證。亦無因果。亦無筋力。亦無相貌。猶如虛空。取不得。捨
不得。山河石壁不能爲礙。出沒往來。自在神通。透五蘊
山。渡生死河。一切業拘此法身不得。此心微妙難見。此
心不同色心。此心是人皆欲得見。於此光明中運手動
足者。如恒河沙。及乎問著。總道不得。猶如木人相似。總
是自己受用。因何不識。佛言。一切衆生盡是迷人。因此

And is what you're doing and saying different from you?

No, it isn't.

But if it isn't, then this body is your real body. And this real body is your mind. And this mind, through endless kalpas without beginning, has never varied. It has never lived or died, appeared or disappeared, increased or decreased. It's not pure or impure, good or evil, past or future. It's not true or false. It's not male or female. It doesn't appear as a monk or a layman, an elder or a novice, a sage or a fool, a buddha or a mortal. It strives for no realization and suffers no karma. It has no strength or form. It's like space. You can't possess it and you can't lose it. Its movements can't be blocked by mountains, rivers, or rock walls. Its unstoppable powers penetrate the Mountain of Five Skandhas[28] and cross the River of Samsara.[29] No karma can restrain this real body. But this mind is subtle and hard to see. It's not the same as the sensual mind. Everyone wants to see this mind, and those who move their hands and feet by its light are as many as the grains of sand along the Ganges, but when you ask them, they can't explain it. They're like puppets. It's theirs to use. Why don't they see it?

The Buddha said people are deluded. This is why when they

作業。墮生死河。欲出還沒。只爲不見性。衆生若不迷。因何問著其中事。無有一人得會者。自家運手動足。因何不識。故知聖人語不錯。迷人自不會曉。故知此難明。惟佛一人能會此法。餘人天及衆生等。盡不明了。若智慧明了。此心號名法性。亦名解脫。生死不拘。一切法拘它不得。是名大自在王如來。亦名不思議。亦名聖體。亦名長生不死。亦名大仙。名雖不同。體卽是一。聖人種種分別。皆不離自心。心量廣大。應用無窮。應眼見色。應耳聞聲。應鼻嗅香。應舌知味。乃至施爲運動。皆是自心。一切時中但有語言道斷。卽是自心。故云如來色無盡。智慧亦復然。色無盡是自心。心識善能分別一切。乃至施爲

act they fall into the River of Endless Rebirth. And when they try to get out, they only sink deeper. And all because they don't see their nature. If people weren't deluded, why would they ask about something right in front of them? Not one of them understands the movement of his own hands and feet. The Buddha wasn't mistaken. Deluded people don't know who they are. Something so hard to fathom is known by a buddha and no one else. Only the wise know this mind, this mind called dharma-nature, this mind called liberation. Neither life nor death can restrain this mind. Nothing can. It's also called the Unstoppable Tathagata,[30] the Incomprehensible, the Sacred Self, the Immortal, the Great Sage. Its names vary but not its essence. Buddhas vary too, but none leaves his own mind.

The mind's capacity is limitless, and its manifestations are inexhaustible. Seeing forms with your eyes, hearing sounds with your ears, smelling odors with your nose, tasting flavors with your tongue, every movement or state is all your mind. At every moment, where language can't go, that's your mind.

The sutras say, "A tathagata's forms are endless. And so is his awareness." The endless variety of forms is due to the mind. Its ability to distinguish things, whatever their movement or state, is

運動皆是智慧心無形相智慧亦無盡故云如來色無盡智慧亦復然四大色身卽是煩惱色身卽有生滅法身常住無所住如來法身常不變異故經云衆生應知佛性本自有之迦葉只是悟得本性本性卽是心心卽是性性卽此同諸佛心前佛後佛只傳此心除此心外無佛可得顚倒衆生不知自心是佛向外馳求終日忙忙念佛禮佛佛在何處不應作如是等見但知自心心外更無別佛經云凡所有相皆是虛妄又云所在之處卽爲有佛自心是佛不應將佛禮佛但是有佛及菩薩相貌忽爾見前切不用禮敬我心空寂本無如是相皃若取相卽是魔盡落邪道若是幻從心起卽不用禮禮

the mind's awareness. But the mind has no form and its awareness no limit. Hence it's said, "A tathagata's forms are endless. And so is his awareness."

A material body of the four elements[31] is trouble. A material body is subject to birth and death. But the real body exists without existing, because a tathagata's real body never changes. The sutras say, "People should realize that the buddha-nature is something they have always had." Kashyapa[32] only realized his own nature.

Our nature is the mind. And the mind is our nature. This nature is the same as the mind of all buddhas. Buddhas of the past and future only transmit this mind. Beyond this mind there's no buddha anywhere. But deluded people don't realize that their own mind is the buddha. They keep searching outside. They never stop invoking buddhas or worshipping buddhas and wondering *Where is the buddha?* Don't indulge in such illusions. Just know your mind. Beyond your mind there's no other buddha. The sutras say, "Everything that has form is an illusion." They also say, "Wherever you are, there's a buddha." Your mind is the buddha. Don't use a buddha to worship a buddha.

Even if a buddha or bodhisattva[33] should suddenly appear before you, there's no need for reverence. This mind of ours is empty and contains no such form. Those who hold onto appearances are devils. They fall from the Path. Why worship illusions born of the mind? Those who worship don't know, and those who

者不知。知者不禮。禮被魔攝。恐學人不知。故作是辨。諸佛如來本性體上。都無如是相皃。切須在意。但有異境界。切不用採括。亦莫生怕怖。不要疑惑。我心本來淸淨。何處有如許相皃。乃至天龍夜叉鬼神帝釋梵王等相。亦不用心生敬重。亦莫怕懼。我心本來空寂。一切相皃皆是妄相。但莫取相。若起佛見法見及佛菩薩等相皃。而生敬重。自墮衆生位中。若欲直會。但莫取一切相卽得。更無別語。故經云。凡所有相。皆是虛妄。都無定實。幻無定相。是無常法。但不取相。合它聖意。故經云。離一切相。卽名諸佛。

問曰。因何不得禮佛菩薩等。答曰。天魔波旬阿修羅示

know don't worship. By worshipping you come under the spell of devils. I point this out because I'm afraid you're unaware of it. The basic nature of a buddha has no such form. Keep this in mind, even if something unusual should appear. Don't embrace it, and don't fear it, and don't doubt that your mind is basically pure. Where could there be room for any such form? Also, at the appearance of spirits, demons, or divine beings,[34] conceive neither respect nor fear. Your mind is basically empty. All appearances are illusions. Don't hold on to appearances.

If you envision a buddha, a dharma, or a bodhisattva[35] and conceive respect for them, you relegate yourself to the realm of mortals. If you seek direct understanding, don't hold on to any appearance whatsoever, and you'll succeed. I have no other advice. The sutras say, "All appearances are illusions." They have no fixed existence, no constant form. They're impermanent. Don't cling to appearances, and you'll be of one mind with the Buddha. The sutras say, "That which is free of all form is the buddha."

But why shouldn't we worship buddhas and bodhisattvas?

Devils and demons possess the power of manifestation. They

見神通、皆作得菩薩相兒、種種變化、是外道、總不是佛。佛是自心、莫錯禮拜、佛是西國語、此土云覺性、覺者靈覺、應機接物、揚眉瞬目、運手動足。皆是自己靈覺之性、性卽是心。心卽是佛、佛卽是道、道卽是禪。禪之一字、非凡聖所測、又云。見本性爲禪、若不見本性、卽非禪也。假使說得千經萬論、若不見本性。只是凡夫、非是佛法、至道幽深、不可話會、典教憑何所及、但見本性。一字不識亦得、見性卽是佛。聖體本來清淨、無有雜穢、所有言說、皆是聖人從心起用、用體本來空、名言猶不及、十二部經憑何得及、道本圓成、不用修證、道非聲色、微妙難見。如人飲水、冷暖自知、不可向人說也。唯有如來能知。餘

can create the appearance of bodhisattvas in all sorts of guises. But they're false. None of them are buddhas. The buddha is your own mind. Don't misdirect your worship.

Buddha is Sanskrit for what you call *aware, miraculously aware*. Responding, perceiving, arching your brows, blinking your eyes, moving your hands and feet, it's all your miraculously aware nature. And this nature is the mind. And the mind is the buddha. And the buddha is the path. And the path is zen.[36] But the word *zen* is one that remains a puzzle to both mortals and sages. Seeing your nature is zen. Unless you see your nature, it's not zen.

Even if you can explain thousands of sutras and shastras,[37] unless you see your own nature yours is the teaching of a mortal, not a buddha. The true Way is sublime. It can't be expressed in language. Of what use are scriptures? But someone who sees his own nature finds the Way, even if he can't read a word. Someone who sees his nature is a buddha. And since a buddha's body is intrinsically pure and unsullied, and everything he says is an expression of his mind, being basically empty, a buddha can't be found in words or anywhere in the Twelvefold Canon.

The Way is basically perfect. It doesn't require perfecting. The Way has no form or sound. It's subtle and hard to perceive. It's like when you drink water: you know how hot or cold it is, but you can't tell others. Of that which only a tathagata knows men and gods remain unaware. The awareness of mortals falls short. As long

人天等類。都不覺知。凡夫智不及。所以有執相。不了自心本來空寂。妄執相及一切法。卽墮外道。若知諸法從心生。不應有執。執卽不知。若見本性。十二部經總是閑文字。千經萬論只是明心。言下契會。教將何用。至理絕言。教是語詞。實不是道。道本無言。言說是妄。若夜夢見樓閣宮殿象馬之屬。及樹木叢林池亭如是等相。不得起一念樂著。盡是托生之處。切須在意。臨終之時。不得取相。卽得除障。疑心暫起。卽魔攝。法身本來清淨無受。只緣迷故。不覺不知。因茲故妄受報。所以有樂著。不得自在。只今若悟得本來身心。卽不染習。若從聖入凡。示見種種雜類。自爲衆生。故聖人逆順皆得自在。一切業

as they're attached to appearances, they're unaware that their minds are empty. And by mistakenly clinging to the appearance of things they lose the Way.

If you know that everything comes from the mind, don't become attached. Once attached, you're unaware. But once you see your own nature, the entire Canon becomes so much prose. Its thousands of sutras and shastras only amount to a clear mind. Understanding comes in midsentence. What good are doctrines?

The ultimate Truth is beyond words. Doctrines are words. They're not the Way. The Way is wordless. Words are illusions. They're no different from things that appear in your dreams at night, be they palaces or carriages, forested parks or lakeside pavilions. Don't conceive any delight for such things. They're all cradles of rebirth. Keep this in mind when you approach death. Don't cling to appearances, and you'll break through all barriers. A moment's hesitation and you'll be under the spell of devils. Your real body is pure and impervious. But because of delusions you're unaware of it. And because of this you suffer karma in vain. Wherever you find delight, you find bondage. But once you awaken to your original body and mind,[38] you're no longer bound by attachments.

Anyone who gives up the transcendent for the mundane, in any of its myriad forms, is a mortal. A buddha is someone who finds freedom in good fortune and bad. Such is his power that

拘它不得。聖人久有大威德。一切品類業。被它聖人轉。天堂地獄無奈何它。凡夫神識昏昧。不同聖人。內外明徹。若有疑即不作。作即流浪生死。後悔無相救處。貧窮困苦皆從妄想生。若了是心。遞相勸勉。但無作而作。即入如來知見。初發心人。神識總不定。若夢中頻見異境。輒不用疑。皆是自心起故。不從外來。夢若見光明出現。過於日輪。即餘習頓盡。法界性見。若有此事。即是成道之因。唯自知。不可向人說。或靜園林中行住坐臥。眼見光明。或大或小。莫與人說。亦不得取。亦是自性光明。或夜靜暗中行住坐臥。眼睹光明。與晝無異。不得怪。並是自心欲明顯。或夜夢中見星月分明。亦自心諸緣欲息。

karma can't hold him. No matter what kind of karma, a buddha transforms it. Heaven and hell[39] are nothing to him. But the awareness of a mortal is dim compared to that of a buddha, who penetrates everything, inside and out.

If you're not sure, don't act. Once you act, you wander through birth and death and regret having no refuge. Poverty and hardship are created by false thinking. To understand this mind you have to act without acting. Only then will you see things from a tathagata's perspective.

But when you first embark on the Path, your awareness won't be focused. You're likely to see all sorts of strange, dreamlike scenes. But you shouldn't doubt that all such scenes come from your own mind and nowhere else.

If, as in a dream, you see a light brighter than the sun, your remaining attachments will suddenly come to an end and the nature of reality will be revealed. Such an occurrence serves as the basis for enlightenment. But this is something only you know. You can't explain it to others.

Or if, while you're walking, standing, sitting, or lying in a quiet grove, you see a light, regardless of whether it's bright or dim, don't tell others and don't focus on it. It's the light of your own nature.

Or if, while you're walking, standing, sitting, or lying in the stillness and darkness of night, everything appears as though in daylight, don't be startled. It's your own mind about to reveal itself.

Or if, while you're dreaming at night, you see the moon and stars in all their clarity, it means the workings of your mind are about to end. But don't tell others. And if your dreams aren't clear,

亦不得向人說。夢若昏昏。猶如陰暗中行。亦是自心煩惱障重。亦自知。若見本性。不用讀經念佛。廣學多知無益。神識轉昏。設教只爲標心。若識心。何用看教。若從凡入聖。即須息業養神。隨分過日。若多嗔恚。令性轉與道相違。自賺無益。聖人於生死中。自在出沒隱顯不定。一切業拘它不得。聖人破邪魔。一切衆生但見本性。餘習頓滅。神識不昧。須是直下便會。只在如今。欲眞會道。莫執一切法。息業養神。餘習亦盡。自然明白。不假用功外道不會佛意。用功最多。違背聖意。終日驅驅念佛轉經昏於神性。不免輪迴。佛是閑人。何用驅驅廣求名利。後時何用。但不見性人。讀經念佛。長學精進。六時行道。長

as if you were walking in the dark, it's because your mind is masked by cares. This too is something only you know.

If you see your nature, you don't need to read sutras or invoke buddhas. Erudition and knowledge are not only useless but also cloud your awareness. Doctrines are only for pointing to the mind. Once you see your mind, why pay attention to doctrines?

To go from mortal to buddha, you have to put an end to karma, nurture your awareness, and accept what life brings. If you're always getting angry, you'll turn your nature against the Way. There's no advantage in deceiving yourself. Buddhas move freely through birth and death, appearing and disappearing at will. They can't be restrained by karma or overcome by devils.

Once mortals see their nature, all attachments end. Awareness isn't hidden. But you can only find it right now. It's only now. If you really want to find the Way, don't hold on to anything. Once you put an end to karma and nurture your awareness, any attachments that remain will come to an end. Understanding comes naturally. You don't have to make any effort. But fanatics[40] don't understand what the Buddha meant. And the harder they try, the farther they get from the Sage's meaning. All day long they invoke buddhas and read sutras. But they remain blind to their own divine nature, and they don't escape the Wheel.

A buddha is an idle person. He doesn't run around after fortune and fame. What good are such things in the end? People who don't see their nature and think reading sutras, invoking buddhas, studying long and hard, practicing morning and night, never lying down, or acquiring knowledge is the Dharma,

坐不臥。廣學多聞。以爲佛法。此等衆生。盡是謗佛法人。
前佛後佛。只言見性。諸行無常。若不見性。妄言我得阿
耨菩提。此是大罪人。十大弟子阿難多聞中得第一。於
佛無識。只學多聞。二乘外道皆無識佛。識數修證。墮在
因果中。是衆生業報。不免生死。遠背佛意。卽是謗佛衆
生。殺卻無罪過。經云。闡提人不生信心。殺卻無罪過。若
有信心。此人是佛位人。若不見性。卽不用取次謗佗良
善。自賺無益。善惡歷然。因果分明。天堂地獄只在眼前。
愚人不信。現墮黑暗地獄中。亦不覺不知。只緣業重故。
所以不信。譬如無目人。不信道有光明。縱向伊說亦不
信。只緣盲故。憑何辨得日光。愚人亦復如是。現今墮畜

blaspheme the Dharma. Buddhas of the past and future only talk about seeing your nature. All practices are impermanent. Unless they see their nature, people who claim to have attained unexcelled, complete enlightenment[41] are liars.

Among Shakyamuni's[42] ten greatest disciples, Ananda[43] was foremost in learning. But he didn't know the Buddha. All he did was study and memorize. Arhats[44] don't know the Buddha. All they know are so many practices for realization, and they become trapped by cause and effect. Such is a mortal's karma: no escape from birth and death. By doing the opposite of what he intended, such people blaspheme the Buddha. Killing them would not be wrong. The sutras say, "Since icchantikas[45] are incapable of belief, killing them would be blameless, whereas people who believe reach the state of buddhahood."

Unless you see your nature, you shouldn't go around criticizing the goodness of others. There's no advantage in deceiving yourself. Good and bad are distinct. Cause and effect are clear. Heaven and hell are right before your eyes. But fools don't believe and fall straight into a hell of endless darkness without even knowing it. What keeps them from believing is the heaviness of their karma. They're like blind people who don't believe there's such a thing as light. Even if you explain it to them, they still don't believe, because they're blind. How can they possibly distinguish light?

The same holds true for fools who end up among the lower

生雜類。誕在貧窮下賤。求生不得。求死不得。雖受是苦。
直問著亦言我今快樂。不異天堂。故知一切衆生。生處
爲樂。亦不覺不知。如斯惡人。只緣業障重故。所以不能
發信心者。不自由它也。若見自心是佛。不在剃除鬚髮。
白衣亦是佛。若不見性。剃除鬚髮。亦是外道。
問曰。白衣有妻子。婬欲不除。憑何得成佛。答曰。只言見
性。不言婬欲。只爲不見性。但得見性。婬欲本來空寂。自
爾斷除。亦不樂著。縱有餘習。不能爲害。何以故。性本清
淨故。雖處在五蘊色身中。其性本來清淨。染污不得。法
身本來無受。無飢無渴。無寒熱。無病。無恩愛。無眷屬。無
苦樂。無好惡。無短長。無强弱。本來無有一物可得。只緣

orders of existence[46] or among the poor and despised. They can't live and they can't die. And despite their sufferings, if you ask them, they say they're as happy as gods. All mortals, even those who think themselves wellborn, are likewise unaware. Because of the heaviness of their karma, such fools can't believe and can't get free.

People who see that their mind is the buddha don't need to shave their head.[47] Laymen are buddhas too. Unless they see their nature, people who shave their head are simply fanatics.

But since married laymen don't give up sex, how can they become buddhas?

I only talk about seeing your nature. I don't talk about sex simply because you don't see your nature. Once you see your nature, sex is basically immaterial. It ends along with your delight in it. Even if some habits remain, they can't harm you, because your nature is essentially pure. Despite dwelling in a material body of four elements, your nature is basically pure. It can't be corrupted. Your real body is basically pure. It can't be corrupted. Your real body has no sensation, no hunger or thirst, no warmth or cold, no sickness, no love or attachment, no pleasure or pain, no good or bad, no shortness or length, no weakness or strength. Actually, there's nothing here. It's only because you cling to this material

執有此色身因卽有飢渴寒熱瘴病等相。若不執。卽一任作。若於生死中得自在。轉一切法。與聖人神通自在無礙。無處不安。若心有疑。決定透一切境界不過。不作最好。作了不免輪迴生死。若見性。旃陀羅亦得成佛。問曰。旃陀羅殺生作業。如何得成佛。答曰。只言見性。不言作業。縱作業不同。一切業拘不得。從無始曠大劫來。只爲不見性。墮地獄中。所以作業輪迴生死。從悟得本性。終不作業。若不見性。念佛免報不得。非論殺生命。若見性疑心頓除。殺生命亦不柰它何。自西天二十七祖。只是遞傳心印。吾今來此土。唯傳頓教大乘。卽心是佛。不言持戒精進苦行。乃至入水火。登於劍輪。一食長坐

body that things like hunger and thirst, warmth and cold, and sickness appear.

Once you stop clinging and let things be, you'll be free, even of birth and death. You'll transform everything. You'll possess spiritual powers[48] that can't be obstructed. And you'll be at peace wherever you are. If you doubt this, you'll never see through anything. You're better off doing nothing. Once you act, you can't avoid the cycle of birth and death. But once you see your nature, you're a buddha even if you work as a butcher.

But butchers create karma by slaughtering animals. How can they be buddhas?

I only talk about seeing your nature. I don't talk about creating karma. Regardless of what we do, our karma has no hold on us. Through endless kalpas without beginning, it's only because people don't see their nature that they end up in hell. As long as a person creates karma, he keeps passing through birth and death. But once a person realizes his original nature, he stops creating karma. If he doesn't see his nature, invoking buddhas won't release him from his karma, regardless of whether or not he's a butcher. But once he sees his nature, all doubts vanish. Even a butcher's karma has no effect on such a person.

In India, the twenty-seven patriarchs[49] only transmitted the imprint[50] of the mind. And the only reason I've come to China is to transmit the instantaneous teaching of the Mahayana:[51] *This mind is the buddha.* I don't talk about precepts, devotions or ascetic practices such as immersing yourself in water and fire, treading a wheel of knives, eating one meal a day, or never lying down. These

不臥。盡是外道有爲法。若識得施爲運動靈覺之性。汝即諸佛心。前佛後佛只言傳心。更無別法。若識此法。凡夫一字不識亦是佛。若不識自己靈覺之性。假使身破如微塵。覓佛終不得也。佛者亦名法身。亦名本心。此心無形相。無因果。無筋骨。猶如虛空。取不得。不同質礙。不同外道。此心除如來一人能會。其餘衆生迷人不明了。此心不離四大色身中。若離是心。即無能運動。是身無知。如草木瓦礫。身是無性。因何運動。若自心動。乃至語言施爲運動。見聞覺知。皆是動心動用。動是心動。動即其用。動用外無心。心外無動。動不是心。心不是動。動本無心。心本無動。動不離心。心不離動。動無心離。心無動

are fanatical, provisional teachings. Once you recognize your moving, miraculously aware nature, yours is the mind of all buddhas. Buddhas of the past and future only talk about transmitting the mind. They teach nothing else. If someone understands this teaching, even if he's illiterate he's a buddha. If you don't see your own miraculously aware nature, you'll never find a buddha even if you break your body into atoms.[52]

The buddha is your real body, your original mind. This mind has no form or characteristics, no cause or effect, no tendons or bones. It's like space. You can't hold it. It's not the mind of materialists or nihilists. Except for a tathagata, no one else—no mortal, no deluded being—can fathom it.

But this mind isn't somewhere outside the material body of four elements. Without this mind we can't move. The body has no awareness. Like a plant or stone, the body has no nature. So how does it move? It's the mind that moves.

Language and behavior, perception and conception are all functions of the moving mind. All motion is the mind's motion. Motion is its function. Apart from motion there's no mind, and apart from the mind there's no motion. But motion isn't the mind. And the mind isn't motion. Motion is basically mindless. And the mind is basically motionless. But motion doesn't exist without the mind. And the mind doesn't exist without motion. There's no mind for motion to exist apart from, and no motion for mind to exist apart from. Motion is the mind's function, and its function is its

離。動是心用。用是心動。動卽心用。用卽心動。不動不用。用體本空。空本無動。動用同心。心本無動。故經云。動而無所動。終日去來而未曾去。終日見而未曾見。終日咲而未曾咲。終日聞而未曾聞。終日知而未曾知。終日喜而未曾喜。終日行而未曾行。終日住而未曾住。故經云。言語道斷。心行處滅。見聞覺知。本自圓寂。乃至嗔喜痛痒何異木人。只緣推尋痛痒不可得。故經云惡業卽得苦報。善業卽有善報。不但嗔墮地獄。喜卽生天。若知嗔喜性空。但不執卽業脫。若不見性。講經決無憑。說亦無盡。略標邪正如是。不及一二也。

達磨大師血脉論終

motion. Even so, the mind neither moves nor functions, because the essence of its functioning is emptiness and emptiness is essentially motionless. Motion is the same as the mind. And the mind is essentially motionless.

Hence the sutras tell us to move without moving, to travel without traveling, to see without seeing, to laugh without laughing, to hear without hearing, to know without knowing, to be happy without being happy, to walk without walking, to stand without standing. And the sutras say, "Go beyond language. Go beyond thought." Basically, seeing, hearing, and knowing are completely empty. Your anger, joy, or pain is like that of a puppet. You can search, but you won't find a thing.

According to the sutras, evil deeds result in hardships and good deeds result in blessings. Angry people go to hell and happy people go to heaven. But once you know that the nature of anger and joy is empty and you let them go, you free yourself from karma. If you don't see your nature, quoting sutras is no help. I could go on, but this brief sermon will have to do.

達磨大師悟性論

夫道者。以寂滅爲體。修者。以離相爲宗。故經云。寂滅是菩提。滅諸相故。佛者覺也。人有覺心。得菩提道。故名爲佛。經云。離一切諸相。卽名諸佛。是知有相。是無相之相。不可以眼見。唯可以智知。若聞此法者。生一念信心。此人以發大乘。超三界。三界者。貪嗔癡是。返貪嗔癡爲戒定慧。卽名超三界。然貪嗔癡亦無實性。但據衆生而言矣。若能返照。了了見貪嗔癡性。卽是佛性。貪嗔癡外。更無別有佛性。經云。諸佛從本來。常處於三毒。長養於白法。而成於世尊。三毒者。貪嗔癡也。言大乘最上乘者。皆

Wake-up Sermon

THE essence of the Way is detachment. And the goal of those who practice is freedom from appearances. The sutras say, "Detachment is enlightenment because it negates appearances." Buddhahood means awareness. Mortals whose minds are aware reach the Way of Enlightenment and are therefore called buddhas. The sutras say, "Those who free themselves from all appearances are called buddhas." The appearance of appearance as no appearance can't be seen visually but can only be known by means of wisdom. Whoever hears and believes this teaching embarks on the Great Vehicle[53] and leaves the three realms.

The three realms are greed, anger, and delusion. To leave the three realms means to go from greed, anger, and delusion back to morality, meditation, and wisdom. Greed, anger, and delusion have no nature of their own. They depend on mortals. And anyone capable of reflection is bound to see that the nature of greed, anger, and delusion is the buddha-nature. Beyond greed, anger, and delusion there is no other buddha-nature. The sutras say, "Buddhas have only become buddhas while living with the three poisons and nourishing themselves on the pure Dharma." The three poisons are greed, anger, and delusion.

The Great Vehicle is the greatest of all vehicles. It's the

是菩薩所行之處。無所不乘亦無所乘。終日乘未嘗乘。此爲佛乘。經云。無乘爲佛乘也。若人知六根不實。五蘊假名。遍體求之。必無定處。當知此人解佛語。經云。五蘊窟宅名禪院。內照開解卽大乘門。可不明哉。不憶一切法。乃名爲禪定。若了此言者。行住坐臥皆禪定。知心是空。名爲見佛。何以故。十方諸佛皆以無心。不見於心。名爲見佛。捨身不悋。名大布施。離諸動定。名大坐禪。何以故。凡夫一向動。小乘一向定。謂出過凡夫小乘之坐禪。名大坐禪。若作此會者。一切諸相不求自解。一切諸病不治自差。此皆大禪定力。凡將心求法者爲迷。不將心求法者爲悟。不著文字名解脫。不染六塵名護法。出離

conveyance of bodhisattvas, who use everything without using anything and who travel all day without traveling. Such is the vehicle of buddhas. The sutras say, "No vehicle is the vehicle of buddhas."

Whoever realizes that the six senses[54] aren't real, that the five aggregates[55] are fictions, that no such things can be located anywhere in the body, understands the language of buddhas. The sutras say, "The cave of five aggregates is the hall of zen. The opening of the inner eye is the door of the Great Vehicle." What could be clearer?

Not thinking about anything is zen. Once you know this, walking, standing, sitting, or lying down, everything you do is zen. To know that the mind is empty is to see the buddha. The buddhas of the ten directions[56] have no mind. To see no mind is to see the buddha.

To give up yourself without regret is the greatest charity. To transcend motion and stillness is the highest meditation. Mortals keep moving, and arhats stay still.[57] But the highest meditation surpasses both that of mortals and that of arhats. People who reach such understanding free themselves from all appearances without effort and cure all illnesses without treatment. Such is the power of great zen.

Using the mind to look for reality is delusion. Not using the mind to look for reality is awareness. Freeing oneself from words is liberation. Remaining unblemished by the dust of sensation is guarding the Dharma. Transcending life and death is leaving home.[58]

生死名出家。不受後有名得道。不生妄想名涅槃。不處無明爲大智慧。無煩惱處名般涅槃。無心相處名爲彼岸。迷時有此岸。若悟時無此岸。何以故。爲凡夫一向住此。若覺最上乘者。心不住此。亦不住彼。故能離於此彼岸也。若見彼岸異於此岸。此人之心。已得無禪定。煩惱名衆生。悟解名菩提。亦不一不異。只隔具迷悟耳。迷時有世間可出。悟時無世間可出。平等法中。不見凡夫異於聖人。經云。平等法者。凡夫不能入。聖人不能行。平等法者。唯有大菩薩與諸佛如來行也。若見生異於死。動異於靜。皆名不平等。不見煩惱異於涅槃。是名平等。何以故。煩惱與涅槃同是一性空故。是以小乘人妄斷煩

Not suffering another existence is reaching the Way. Not creating delusions is enlightenment. Not engaging in ignorance is wisdom. No affliction is nirvana. And no appearance of the mind is the other shore.

When you're deluded, this shore exists. When you wake up, it doesn't exist. Mortals stay on this shore. But those who discover the greatest of all vehicles stay on neither this shore nor the other shore. They're able to leave both shores. Those who see the other shore as different from this shore don't understand zen.

Delusion means mortality. And awareness means buddhahood. They're not the same. And they're not different. It's just that people distinguish delusion from awareness. When we're deluded there's a world to escape. When we're aware, there's nothing to escape.

In the light of the impartial Dharma, mortals look no different from sages. The sutras say that the impartial Dharma is something that mortals can't penetrate and sages can't practice. The impartial Dharma is only practiced by great bodhisattvas and buddhas. To look on life as different from death or on motion as different from stillness is to be partial. To be impartial means to look on suffering as no different from nirvana, because the nature of both is emptiness. By imagining they're putting an end to suffering and entering nirvana arhats end up trapped by nirvana. But bodhisattvas know

惱妄入涅槃。爲涅槃所滯。菩薩知煩惱性空。卽不離空。
故常在涅槃。涅槃者。涅而不生。槃而不死。出離生死。出
般涅槃。心無去來。卽入涅槃。是知涅槃卽是空心。諸佛
入涅槃者。爲在無妄想處。菩薩入道場者。卽是無煩惱
處。空閑處者。卽是無貪嗔癡也。貪爲欲界。嗔爲色界。癡
爲無色界。若一念心生。卽入三界。一念心滅。卽出三界。
是知三界生滅。萬法有無。皆由一心。凡言一法者。似破
瓦石竹木無情之物。若知心是假名。無有實體。卽知自
家之心亦是非有。亦是非無。何以故。凡夫一向生心。名
爲有。小乘一向滅心。名爲無。菩薩與佛未曾生心。未曾
滅心。名爲非有非無心。非有非無心。此名爲中道。是知

that suffering is essentially empty. And by remaining in emptiness they remain in nirvana. Nirvana means no birth and no death. It's beyond birth and death and beyond nirvana. When the mind stops moving, it enters nirvana. Nirvana is an empty mind. Where delusions don't exist, buddhas reach nirvana. Where afflictions don't exist, bodhisattvas enter the place of enlightenment.[59]

An uninhabited place[60] is one without greed, anger, or delusion. Greed is the realm of desire, anger the realm of form, and delusion the formless realm. When a thought begins, you enter the three realms. When a thought ends, you leave the three realms. The beginning or end of the three realms, the existence or nonexistence of anything, depends on the mind. This applies to everything, even to such inanimate objects as rocks and sticks.

Whoever knows that the mind is a fiction and devoid of anything real knows that his own mind neither exists nor doesn't exist. Mortals keep creating the mind, claiming it exists. And arhats keep negating the mind, claiming it doesn't exist. But bodhisattvas and buddhas neither create nor negate the mind. This is what's meant by the mind that neither exists nor doesn't exist. The mind that neither exists nor doesn't exist is called the Middle Way.[61]

持心學法則心法俱迷不持心學法則心法俱悟凡迷者迷於悟悟者悟於迷正見之人知心空無卽超迷悟無有迷悟始名正解正見色不自色由心故色心不自心由色故心是知心色兩相俱生滅有者有於無無者無於有是名眞見夫眞見者無所不見亦無所見見滿十方未曾有見何以故無所見故見無見故見非見故凡夫所見皆名妄想若寂滅無見始名眞見心境相對見生於中若內不起心則外不生境境心俱淨乃名爲眞見作此解時乃名正解不見一切法乃名得道不解一切法乃名解法何以故見與不見俱不見故解與不解俱不解故無見之見乃名眞見無解之解乃名大解

If you use your mind to study reality, you won't understand either your mind or reality. If you study reality without using your mind, you'll understand both. Those who don't understand, don't understand understanding. And those who understand, understand not understanding. People capable of true vision[62] know that the mind is empty. They transcend both understanding and not understanding. The absence of both understanding and not understanding is true understanding.

Seen with true vision, form isn't simply form, because form depends on mind. And mind isn't simply mind, because mind depends on form. Mind and form create and negate each other. That which exists exists in relation to that which doesn't exist. And that which doesn't exist doesn't exist in relation to that which exists. This is true vision. By means of such vision nothing is seen and nothing is not seen. Such vision reaches throughout the ten directions without seeing: because nothing is seen; because not seeing is seen; because seeing isn't seeing. What mortals see are delusions. True vision is detached from seeing.

The mind and the world are opposites, and vision arises where they meet. When your mind doesn't stir inside, the world doesn't arise outside. When the world and the mind are both transparent, this is true vision. And such understanding is true understanding.

To see nothing is to perceive the Way, and to understand nothing is to know the Dharma, because seeing is neither seeing nor not seeing and because understanding is neither understanding nor not understanding. Seeing without seeing is true vision. Understanding without understanding is true understanding.

夫正見者。非直見於見。亦乃見於不見。眞解者。非直解於解。亦乃解於無解。凡有所解。皆名不解。無所解者。始名正解。解與不解。俱非解也。經云。不捨智慧名愚癡。以心爲空。解與不解俱是眞。以心爲有。解與不解俱是妄。若解時法逐人。若不解時人逐法。若法逐於人。則非法成法。若人逐於法。則法成非法。若人逐於法。則法皆妄。若法逐於人。則法皆眞。是以聖人亦不將心求法。亦不將法求心。亦不將心求心。亦不將法求法。所以心不生法。法不生心。心法兩寂。故常爲在定。衆生心生。則佛法滅。衆生心滅。則佛法生。心生則眞法滅。心滅則眞法生。已知一切法各各不相屬。是名得道人。知心不屬一切

True vision isn't just seeing seeing. It's also seeing not seeing. And true understanding isn't just understanding understanding. It's also understanding not understanding. If you understand anything, you don't understand. Only when you understand nothing is it true understanding. Understanding is neither understanding nor not understanding.

The sutras say, "Not to let go of wisdom is stupidity." When the mind doesn't exist, understanding and not understanding are both true. When the mind exists, understanding and not understanding are both false.

When you understand, reality depends on you. When you don't understand, you depend on reality. When reality depends on you, that which isn't real becomes real. When you depend on reality, that which is real becomes false. When you depend on reality, everything is false. When reality depends on you, everything is true. Thus, the sage doesn't use his mind to look for reality, or reality to look for his mind, or his mind to look for his mind, or reality to look for reality. His mind doesn't give rise to reality. And reality doesn't give rise to his mind. And because both his mind and reality are still, he's always in samadhi.[63]

When the mortal mind appears, buddhahood disappears. When the mortal mind disappears, buddhahood appears. When the mind appears, reality disappears. When the mind disappears, reality appears. Whoever knows that nothing depends on anything has found the Way. And whoever knows that the mind depends on nothing is always at the place of enlightenment.

法此人常在道場迷時有罪。解時無罪。何以故罪性空故若迷時無罪見罪。若解時即罪非罪。何以故。罪無處所故。經云。諸法無性。直用莫疑。疑即成罪。何以故。罪因疑惑而生。若作此解者。前世罪業即爲消滅迷時六識五陰皆是煩惱生死法。悟時六識五陰皆是涅槃無生死法。修道人不外求道。何以故。知心是道若得心時。無心可得。若得道時。無道可得。若言將心求道得者。皆名邪見。迷時有佛有法。悟無佛無法。何以故悟即是佛法。夫修道者。身滅道成。亦如甲折樹生。此業報身。念念無常。無一定法。但隨念修之。亦不得厭生死。亦不得愛生死。但念念之中。不得妄想。則生證有餘涅槃。死入無生

When you don't understand, you're wrong. When you understand, you're not wrong. This is because the nature of wrong is empty. When you don't understand, right seems wrong. When you understand, wrong isn't wrong, because wrong doesn't exist. The sutras say, "Nothing has a nature of its own." Act. Don't question. When you question, you're wrong. Wrong is the result of questioning. When you reach such an understanding, the wrong deeds of your past lives are wiped away. When you're deluded, the six senses and five shades[64] are constructs of suffering and mortality. When you wake up, the six senses and five shades are constructs of nirvana and immortality.

Someone who seeks the Way doesn't look beyond himself. He knows that the mind is the Way. But when he finds the mind, he finds nothing. And when he finds the Way, he finds nothing. If you think you can use the mind to find the Way, you're deluded. When you're deluded, buddhahood exists. When you're aware, it doesn't exist. This is because awareness is buddhahood.

If you're looking for the Way, the Way won't appear until your body disappears. It's like stripping bark from a tree. This karmic body undergoes constant change. It has no fixed reality. Practice according to your thoughts. Don't hate life and death or love life and death. Keep your every thought free of delusion, and in life you'll witness the beginning of nirvana,[65] and in death you'll experience the assurance of no rebirth.[66]

法忍。眼見色時。不染於色。耳聞聲時。不染於聲。皆解脫
也。眼不著色。眼爲禪門。耳不著聲。耳爲禪門。總而言。見
色有見色性不著。常解脫。見色相者常繫縛。不爲煩惱
所繫縛者。卽名解脫。更無別解脫。善觀色者。色不生心。
心不生色。卽色與心俱清淨。無妄想時。一心是一佛國。
有妄想時。一心是一地獄。衆生造作妄想。以心生心。故
常在地獄。菩薩觀察妄想。不以心生心。常在佛國。若不
以心生心。則心心入空。念念歸靜。從一佛國至一佛國。
若以心生心。則心心不靜。念念歸動。從一地獄歷一地
獄。若一念心起。則有善惡二業。有天堂地獄。若一念心
不起。卽無善惡二業。亦無天堂地獄。爲體非有非無。在

To see form but not be corrupted by form or to hear sound but not be corrupted by sound is liberation. Eyes that aren't attached to form are the Gates of Zen. Ears that aren't attached to sound are also the Gates of Zen. In short, those who perceive the existence and nature of phenomena and remain unattached are liberated. Those who perceive the external appearance of phenomena are at their mercy. Not to be subject to affliction is what's meant by liberation. There's no other liberation. When you know how to look at form, form doesn't give rise to mind and mind doesn't give rise to form. Form and mind are both pure.

When delusions are absent, the mind is the land of buddhas. When delusions are present, the mind is hell. Mortals create delusions. And by using the mind to give birth to mind they always find themselves in hell. Bodhisattvas see through delusions. And by not using the mind to give birth to mind they always find themselves in the land of buddhas. If you don't use your mind to create mind, every state of mind is empty and every thought is still. You go from one buddha-land[67] to another. If you use your mind to create mind, every state of mind is disturbed and every thought is in motion. You go from one hell to the next. When a thought arises, there's good karma and bad karma, heaven and hell. When no thought arises, there's no good karma or bad karma, no heaven or hell.

The body neither exists nor doesn't exist. Hence existence as

凡卽有在聖卽無聖人無其心。故胸臆空洞。與天同量。

此已下並是大道中證。非小乘及凡夫境界也。心得涅槃時。卽不見有涅槃。何以故。心是涅槃。若心外更見涅槃。此名著邪見也。一切煩惱爲如來種心。爲因煩惱而得智慧。只可道煩惱生如來。不可得道煩惱是如來。故身心爲田疇。煩惱爲種子。智慧爲萌牙。如來喻於穀也。佛在心中。如香在樹中。煩惱若盡。佛從心出。朽腐若盡。香從樹出。卽知樹外無香。心外無佛。若樹外有香。卽是他香。心外有佛。卽是他佛。心中有三毒者。是名國土穢惡。心中無三毒者。是名國土清淨。經云。若使國土不淨。穢惡充滿。諸佛世尊於中出者。無有此事。不淨穢惡者。

a mortal and nonexistence as a sage are conceptions with which a sage has nothing to do. His heart is empty and spacious as the sky.

That which follows is witnessed on the Way. It's beyond the ken of arhats and mortals.

When the mind reaches nirvana, you don't see nirvana, because the mind is nirvana. If you see nirvana somewhere outside the mind, you're deluding yourself.

Every suffering is a buddha-seed, because suffering impels mortals to seek wisdom. But you can only say that suffering gives rise to buddhahood. You can't say that suffering is buddhahood. Your body and mind are the field. Suffering is the seed, wisdom the sprout, and buddhahood the grain.

The buddha in the mind is like a fragrance in a tree. The buddha comes from a mind free of suffering, just as a fragrance comes from a tree free of decay. There's no fragrance without the tree and no buddha without the mind. If there's a fragrance without a tree, it's a different fragrance. If there's a buddha without your mind, it's a different buddha.

When the three poisons are present in your mind, you live in a land of filth. When the three poisons are absent from your mind, you live in a land of purity. The sutras say, "If you fill a land with impurity and filth, no buddha will ever appear." Impurity and filth

卽無明三毒是諸佛世尊者卽淸淨覺悟心是一切言語無非佛法若能無其所言而盡日言是道若能有其所言卽終日默而非道是故如來言不乘默默不乘言言不離默悟此言默者皆在三昧若知時而言言亦解脫若不知時而默默亦繫縛是故言若離相言亦名解脫默若著相默卽是繫縛夫文字者本性解脫文字不能就繫縛繫縛自本來未就文字法無高下若見高下非法也非法爲筏是法爲人筏者人乘其筏者卽得渡於非法則是法也若世俗言卽有男女貴賤以道言之卽無男女貴賤以是天女悟道不變女形車匿解眞寧移賤稱乎此蓋非男女貴賤皆由一相也天女於十二

refer to delusion and the other poisons. A buddha refers to a pure and awakened mind.

There's no language that isn't the Dharma. To talk all day without saying anything is the Way. To be silent all day and still say something isn't the Way. Hence neither does a tathagata's speech depend on silence, nor does his silence depend on speech, nor does his speech exist apart from his silence. Those who understand both speech and silence are in samadhi. If you speak when you know, your speech is free. If you're silent when you don't know, your silence is tied. If speech isn't attached to appearances, it's free. If silence is attached to appearances, it's tied. Language is essentially free. It has nothing to do with attachment. And attachment has nothing to do with language.

Reality has no high or low. If you see high or low, it isn't real. A raft[68] isn't real. But a passenger raft is. A person who rides such a raft can cross that which isn't real. That's why it's real.

According to the world there's male and female, rich and poor. According to the Way there's no male or female, no rich or poor. When the goddess realized the Way, she didn't change her sex. When the stable boy[69] awakened to the Truth, he didn't change his status. Free of sex and status, they shared the same basic appearance. The goddess searched twelve years for her womanhood

年中。求女相了不可得。卽知於十二年中。求男相亦不可得。十二年者卽十二入是也。離心無佛。離佛無心。亦如離水無冰。亦如離冰無水。凡言離心者。非是遠離於心。但使不著心相。經云。不見相。名爲見佛。卽是離心相也。離心無佛者。言佛從心出。心能生佛。然佛從心生。而心未嘗生於佛。亦如魚生於水。水不生於魚。欲觀於魚未見魚。而先見水。欲觀佛者。未見佛。而先見心。卽知已見魚者。忘於水。已見佛者。忘於心。若不忘於心。尚爲心所惑。若不忘於水。尚被水所迷。衆生與菩提。亦如冰之與水。爲三毒所燒。卽名衆生。爲三解脫所淨。卽名菩提。爲三冬、所凍。卽名爲冰。爲三夏所消。卽名爲水。若捨卻

without success. To search twelve years for one's manhood would likewise be fruitless. The twelve years refer to the twelve entrances.[70]

Without the mind there's no buddha. Without the buddha there's no mind. Likewise, without water there's no ice, and without ice there's no water. Whoever talks about leaving the mind doesn't get very far. Don't become attached to appearances of the mind. The sutras say, "When you see no appearance, you see the buddha." This is what's meant by being free from appearances of the mind.

Without the mind there's no buddha means that the buddha comes from the mind. The mind gives birth to the buddha. But although the buddha comes from the mind, the mind doesn't come from the buddha, just as fish come from water, but water doesn't come from fish. Whoever wants to see a fish sees the water before he sees the fish. And whoever wants to see a buddha sees the mind before he sees the buddha. Once you've seen the fish, you forget about the water. And once you've seen the buddha, you forget about the mind. If you don't forget about the mind, the mind will confuse you, just as the water will confuse you if you don't forget about it.

Mortality and buddhahood are like water and ice. To be afflicted by the three poisons is mortality. To be purified by the three releases[71] is buddhahood. That which freezes into ice in winter melts into water in summer. Eliminate ice and there's no

冰。卽無別水。若棄卻衆生則無別菩提。明知冰性卽是水性。水性卽是氷性。衆生性者。卽菩提性也。衆生與菩提同一性。亦如烏頭與附子共根耳。但時節不同。迷異境故。有衆生菩提二名矣。是以蛇化爲龍。不改其鱗。凡變爲聖。不改其面。但知心者智內照。身者戒外眞。衆生度佛。佛度衆生。是名平等。衆生度佛者。煩惱生悟解。佛度衆生者。悟解滅煩惱。是知非無煩惱。非無悟解。是知非煩惱無以生悟解。非悟解無以滅煩惱。若迷時佛度衆生。若悟時衆生度佛。何以故。佛不自成。皆由衆生度故。諸佛以無明爲父。貪愛爲母。無明貪愛皆是衆生別名也。衆生與無明亦如左掌與右掌。更無別也。迷時在

more water. Get rid of mortality and there's no more buddhahood. Clearly, the nature of ice is the nature of water. And the nature of water is the nature of ice. And the nature of mortality is the nature of buddhahood. Mortality and buddhahood share the same nature, just as wutou and futzu[72] share the same root but not the same season. It's only because of the delusion of differences that we have the words *mortality* and *buddhahood*. When a snake becomes a dragon, it doesn't change its scales. And when a mortal becomes a sage, he doesn't change his face. He knows his mind through internal wisdom and takes care of his body through external discipline.

Mortals liberate buddhas and buddhas liberate mortals. This is what's meant by impartiality. Mortals liberate buddhas because affliction creates awareness. And buddhas liberate mortals because awareness negates affliction. There can't help but be affliction. And there can't help but be awareness. If it weren't for affliction, there would be nothing to create awareness. And if it weren't for awareness, there would be nothing to negate affliction. When you're deluded, buddhas liberate mortals. When you're aware, mortals liberate buddhas. Buddhas don't become buddhas on their own. They're liberated by mortals. Buddhas regard delusion as their father and greed as their mother. Delusion and greed are different names for mortality. Delusion and mortality are like the left hand and the right hand. There's no other difference.

When you're deluded, you're on this shore. When you're

此岸。悟時在彼岸。若知心空不見相。則離迷悟。既離迷悟。亦無彼岸。如來不在此岸。亦不在彼岸。不在中流。中流者。小乘人也。此岸者。凡夫也。彼岸菩提也。佛有三身者。化身報身法身。化身亦云應身。若衆生現作善時卽化身。現修智慧時卽報身。現覺無爲卽法身。常現飛騰十方隨宜救濟者。化身佛也。若斷惑卽是雪山成道。報身佛也。無言無說。無作無得。湛然常住。法身佛也。若論至理一佛尙無。何得有三。此謂三身者但據人智也。人有上中下說。下智之人妄興福力也。妄見化身佛。中智之人妄斷煩惱。妄見報身佛。上智之人妄證菩提。妄見法身佛。上上智之人內照圓寂。明心卽佛。不待心而

aware, you're on the other shore. But once you know your mind is empty and you see no appearances, you're beyond delusion and awareness. And once you're beyond delusion and awareness, the other shore doesn't exist. The tathagata isn't on this shore or the other shore. And he isn't in midstream. Arhats are in midstream and mortals are on this shore. On the other shore is buddhahood.

Buddhas have three bodies:[73] a transformation body, a reward body, and a real body. The transformation body is also called the incarnation body. The transformation body appears when mortals do good deeds, the reward body when they cultivate wisdom, and the real body when they become aware of the sublime. The transformation body is the one you see flying in all directions rescuing others wherever it can. The reward body puts an end to doubts. *The Great Enlightenment occurred in the Himalayas*[74] suddenly becomes true. The real body doesn't do or say anything. It remains perfectly still. But actually, there's not even one buddha-body, much less three. This talk of three bodies is simply based on human understanding, which can be shallow, moderate, or deep.

People of shallow understanding imagine they're piling up blessings and mistake the transformation body for the buddha. People of moderate understanding imagine they're putting an end to suffering and mistake the reward body for the buddha. And people of deep understanding imagine they're experiencing buddhahood and mistake the real body for the buddha. But people of the deepest understanding look within, distracted by nothing. Since a clear mind is the buddha, they attain the understanding of a buddha without using the mind. The three bodies, like all other things, are

得佛智。知三身與萬法皆不可取不可說。此卽解脫心。成於大道。經云。佛不說法。不度衆生。不證菩提。此之謂矣。衆生造業。業不造衆生。今世造業。後世受報。無有脫時。唯有至人。於此身中。不造諸業。故不受報。經云。諸業不造。自然得道。豈虛言哉。人能造業。今不能造人。人若造業。業與人俱生。人若不造業。業與人俱滅。是知業由人造。人由業生。人若不造業。卽業無由生人也。亦如人能弘道。道不能弘人。今之凡夫。往往造業。妄說無報。豈至少不苦哉。若以至少而理。前心造。後心報。何有脫時。若前心不造。卽後心無報。復安妄見業報。經云。雖信有佛。言佛苦行。是名邪見。雖信有佛。言佛有金鏘馬麥之

unattainable and indescribable. The unimpeded mind reaches the Way. The sutras say, "Buddhas don't preach the Dharma. They don't liberate mortals. And they don't experience buddhahood." This is what I mean.

Individuals create karma; karma doesn't create individuals. They create karma in this life and receive their reward in the next. They never escape. Only someone who's perfect creates no karma in this life and receives no reward. The sutras say, "Who creates no karma obtains the Dharma." This isn't an empty saying. You can create karma, but you can't create a person. When you create karma, you're reborn along with your karma. When you don't create karma, you vanish along with your karma. Hence, with karma dependent on the individual and the individual dependent on karma, if an individual doesn't create karma, karma has no hold on him. In the same manner, "A person can enlarge the Way. The Way can't enlarge a person."[75]

Mortals keep creating karma and mistakenly insist that there's no retribution. But can they deny suffering? Can they deny that what the present state of mind sows the next state of mind reaps? How can they escape? But if the present state of mind sows nothing, the next state of mind reaps nothing. Don't misconceive karma.

The sutras say, "Despite believing in buddhas, people who imagine that buddhas practice austerities aren't Buddhists. The same holds for those who imagine that buddhas are subject to

報。是名信不具足。是名一闡提。解聖法名爲聖人。解凡法者名爲凡夫。但能捨凡法就聖法。卽凡夫成聖人矣。世間愚人。但欲遠求聖人。不信慧解之心爲聖人也。經云。無智人中莫說此經。經云心也法也。無智之人。不信此心。解法成於聖人。但欲遠外求學。愛慕空中佛像光明香色等事。皆墮邪見。失心狂亂。經云。若見諸相非相。卽見如來。八萬四千法門。盡由一心而起。若心相內淨。猶如虛空。卽出離身心內。八萬四千煩惱。爲病本也。凡夫當生憂死。飽臨愁飢。皆名大惑。所以聖人不謀其前。不慮其後。無戀當今。念念歸道。若未悟此大理者。卽須早求人天之善。無令兩失。

達磨大師悟性論終

rewards of wealth or poverty. They're icchantikas. They're incapable of belief."

Someone who understands the teaching of sages is a sage. Someone who understands the teaching of mortals is a mortal. A mortal who can give up the teaching of mortals and follow the teaching of sages becomes a sage. But the fools of this world prefer to look for sages far away. They don't believe that the wisdom of their own mind is the sage. The sutras say, "Among men of no understanding, don't preach this sutra." And the sutras say, "Mind is the teaching." But people of no understanding don't believe in their own mind or that by understanding this teaching they can become a sage. They prefer to look for distant knowledge and long for things in space, buddha-images, light, incense, and colors. They fall prey to falsehood and lose their minds to insanity.

The sutras say, "When you see that all appearances are not appearances, you see the tathagata." The myriad doors to the truth all come from the mind. When appearances of the mind are as transparent as space, they're gone.

Our endless sufferings are the roots of illness. When mortals are alive, they worry about death. When they're full, they worry about hunger. Theirs is the Great Uncertainty. But sages don't consider the past. And they don't worry about the future. Nor do they cling to the present. And from moment to moment they follow the Way. If you haven't awakened to this great truth, you'd better look for a teacher on earth or in the heavens. Don't compound your own deficiency.

達磨大師破相論

論曰。若復有人志求佛道者。當修何法最爲省要。答曰。唯觀心一法總攝諸法最爲省要。問曰。何一法能攝諸法。答曰。心者萬法之根本。一切諸法唯心所生。若能了心。則萬法俱備。猶如大樹。所有枝條及諸花果。皆悉依根。栽樹者。存根而始生子。伐樹者。去根而必死。若了心修道。則少力而易成。不了心而修。費功而無益。故知一切善惡皆由自心。心外別求。終無是處。

問曰。云何觀心稱之爲了。答菩薩摩訶薩。行深般若波羅蜜多時。了四大五陰本空無我。了見自心起用。有二

Breakthrough Sermon

IF someone is determined to reach enlightenment, what is the most essential method he can practice?

The most essential method, which includes all other methods, is beholding the mind.

But how can one method include all others?

The mind is the root from which all things grow. If you can understand the mind, everything else is included. It's like the root of a tree. All a tree's fruit and flowers, branches and leaves depend on its root. If you nourish its root, a tree multiplies. If you cut its root, it dies. Those who understand the mind reach enlightenment with minimal effort. Those who don't understand the mind practice in vain. Everything good and bad comes from your own mind. To find something beyond the mind is impossible.

But how can beholding the mind be called understanding?

When a great bodhisattva delves deeply into perfect wisdom,[76] he realizes that the four elements and five shades are devoid of a personal self. And he realizes that the activity of his mind has two aspects: pure and impure.[77] By their very nature, these two mental

種差別。云何爲二。一者淨心。二者染心。此二種心法。亦自然本來俱有。雖假緣合。互相因待。淨心恒樂善因。染心常思惡業。若不受所染。則稱之爲聖。遂能遠離諸苦。證涅槃樂。若墮染心。造業受其纏覆。則名之爲凡。沉淪三界。受種種苦。何以故。由彼染心。障眞如體故。十地經云。衆生身中有金剛佛性。猶如日輪。體明圓滿。廣大無邊。只爲五陰重雲所覆。如缾內燈光。不能顯現。又涅槃經云。一切衆生悉有佛性。無明覆故。不得解脫。佛性者。即覺性也。但自覺覺他。覺知明了。則名解脫。故知一切諸善。以覺爲根。因其覺根。遂能顯現諸功德樹。涅槃之果德。因此而成。如是觀心。可名爲了。

states are always present. They alternate as cause or effect depending on conditions, the pure mind delighting in good deeds, the impure mind thinking of evil. Those who aren't affected by impurity are sages. They transcend suffering and experience the bliss of nirvana. All others, trapped by the impure mind and entangled by their own karma, are mortals. They drift through the three realms and suffer countless afflictions, and all because their impure mind obscures their real self.

The *Sutra of Ten Stages* says, "In the body of mortals is the indestructible buddha-nature. Like the sun, its light fills endless space. But once veiled by the dark clouds of the five shades, it's like a light inside a jar, hidden from view." And the *Nirvana Sutra*[78] says, "All mortals have the buddha-nature. But it's covered by darkness from which they can't escape. Our buddha-nature is awareness: to be aware and to make others aware. To realize awareness is liberation." Everything good has awareness for its root. And from this root of awareness grow the tree of all virtues and the fruit of nirvana. Beholding the mind like this is understanding.

問上說眞如佛性一切功德因覺爲根未審無明之心以何爲根答無明之心雖有八萬四千煩惱情欲及恒河沙眾惡皆因三毒以爲根本其三毒者貪嗔癡是也此三毒心自能具足一切諸惡猶如大樹根雖是一所生枝葉其數無邊彼三毒根一一根中生諸惡業百千萬億倍過於前不可爲喻如是三毒心於本體中應現六根亦名六賊即六識也由此六識出入諸根貪著萬境能成惡業障眞如體故名六賊一切眾生由此三毒六賊惑亂身心沈沒生死輪迴六趣受諸苦惱猶如江河因小泉源洎流不絕乃能彌漫波濤萬里若復有人斷其本源即眾流皆息求解脫者能轉三毒爲三聚淨

You say that our true buddha-nature and all virtues have awareness for their root. But what is the root of ignorance?

The ignorant mind, with its infinite afflictions, passions, and evils, is rooted in the three poisons: greed, anger, and delusion. These three poisoned states of mind themselves include countless evils, like trees that have a single trunk but countless branches and leaves. Yet each poison produces so many more millions of evils that the example of a tree is hardly a fitting comparison.

The three poisons are present in our six sense organs[79] as six kinds of consciousness,[80] or thieves. They're called thieves because they pass in and out of the gates of the senses, covet limitless possessions, engage in evil, and mask their true identity. And because mortals are misled in body and mind by these poisons or thieves, they become lost in life and death, wander through the six states of existence,[81] and suffer countless afflictions. These afflictions are like rivers that surge for a thousand miles because of the constant flow of small springs. But if someone cuts off their source, rivers dry up. And if someone who seeks liberation can turn the three poisons into the three sets of precepts and the six thieves into

戒。轉六賊爲六波羅蜜。自然永離一切諸苦。
問。六趣三界廣大無邊。若唯觀心。何由免無窮之苦。答。
三界業報。唯心所生。本若無心。於三界中。卽出三界。其
三界者。卽三毒也。貪爲欲界。嗔爲色界。癡爲無色界。故
名三界。由此三毒。造業輕重受報不同。分歸六處。故名
六趣。
問。云何輕重分之爲六。答。衆生不了正因。迷心修善。未
免三界。生三輕趣。云何三輕趣。所謂迷修十善。妄求快
樂。未免貪界。生於天趣。迷持五戒。妄起愛憎。未免瞋界。
生於人趣。迷執有爲。信邪求福。未免癡界。生阿修羅趣。
如是三類。名三輕趣。云何三重。所謂縱三毒心。唯造惡

the six paramitas, he rids himself of affliction once and for all.

But the three realms and six states of existence are infinitely vast. How can we escape their endless afflictions if all we do is behold the mind?

The karma of the three realms comes from the mind alone. If your mind isn't within the three realms, it's beyond them. The three realms correspond to the three poisons: greed corresponds to the realm of desire, anger to the realm of form, and delusion to the formless realm. And because karma created by the poisons can be gentle or heavy, these three realms are further divided into six places known as the six states of existence.

And how does the karma of these six differ?

Mortals who don't understand true practice[82] and blindly perform good deeds are born into the three higher states of existence within the three realms. And what are these three higher states? Those who blindly perform the ten good deeds[33] and foolishly seek happiness are born as gods in the realm of desire. Those who blindly observe the five precepts[84] and foolishly indulge in love and hate are born as men in the realm of anger. And those who blindly cling to the phenomenal world, believe in false doctrines, and pray for blessings are born as demons in the realm of delusion. These are the three higher states of existence.

And what are the three lower states? They're where those who persist in poisoned thoughts and evil deeds are born. Those

業墮三重趣。若貪業重者。墮餓鬼趣。瞋業重者。墮地獄趣。癡業重者。墮畜生趣。如是三重。通前三輕。遂成六趣。故知一切苦業由自心生。但能攝心。離諸邪惡。三界六趣輪迴之苦。自然消滅離苦。卽得解脫。

問。如佛所說。我於三大阿僧祇劫。無量勤苦。方成佛道。云何今說唯只觀心。制三毒。卽名解脫。答。佛所說。言無虛妄也。阿僧祇劫者。卽三毒心也。胡言阿僧祇。漢名不可數。此三毒心於中有恒沙惡念。於一一念中。皆爲一劫。如是恒沙不可數也。故言三大阿僧祇。眞如之性。既被三毒之所覆蓋。若不超彼三大恒沙毒惡之心。云何名爲解脫。今若能轉貪嗔癡等三毒心。爲三解脫。是則

whose karma from greed is greatest become hungry ghosts. Those whose karma from anger is greatest become sufferers in hell. And those whose karma from delusion is greatest become beasts. These three lower states together with the previous three higher states form the six states of existence. From this you should realize that all karma, painful or otherwise, comes from your own mind. If you can just concentrate your mind and transcend its falsehood and evil, the suffering of the three realms and six states of existence will automatically disappear. And once free from suffering, you're truly free.

But the Buddha said, "Only after undergoing innumerable hardships for three asankhya kalpas[85] *did I achieve enlightenment." Why do you now say that simply beholding the mind and overcoming the three poisons is liberation?*

The words of the Buddha are true. But the three asankhya kalpas refer to the three poisoned states of mind. What we call *asankhya* in Sanskrit you call countless. Within these three poisoned states of mind are countless evil thoughts. And every thought lasts a kalpa. Such an infinity is what the Buddha meant by the three asankhya kalpas.

Once your real self becomes obscured by the three poisons, how can you be called liberated until you overcome their countless evil thoughts? People who can transform the three poisons of greed, anger, and delusion into the three releases are said to pass through the three asankhya kalpas. But people of this final age[86] are the

名爲得度三大阿僧祇劫。末世衆生愚癡鈍根。不解如來三大阿僧祇秘密之說。遂言成佛塵劫未期。豈不疑誤行人退菩提道。

問菩薩摩訶薩由持三聚淨戒。行六波羅蜜。方成佛道。今令學者唯只觀心。不修戒行。云何成佛。答。三聚淨戒者。即制三毒心也。制三毒成無量善聚。聚者會也。無量善法普會於心。故名三聚淨戒。六波羅蜜者。即淨六根也。胡名波羅蜜。漢名達彼岸。以六根清淨。不染六塵。即是度煩惱河。至菩提岸。故名六波羅蜜。

問。如經所說。三聚淨戒者。誓斷一切惡。誓修一切善。誓度一切衆生。今者唯言制三毒心。豈不文義有乖也。答。

densest of fools. They don't understand what the Tathagata really meant by the three asankhya kalpas. They say enlightenment is only achieved after endless kalpas and thereby mislead disciples to retreat on the path to buddhahood.

But the great bodhisattvas have achieved enlightenment only by observing the three sets of precepts[87] *and practicing the six paramitas. Now you tell disciples merely to behold the mind. How can anyone reach enlightenment without cultivating the rules of discipline?*

The three sets of precepts are for overcoming the three poisoned states of mind. When you overcome these poisons, you create three sets of limitless virtue. A set gathers things together—in this case, countless good thoughts throughout your mind. And the six paramitas are for purifying the six senses. What we call *paramitas* you call *means to the other shore*.[88] By purifying your six senses of the dust of sensation, the paramitas ferry you across the River of Affliction to the Shore of Enlightenment.

According to the sutras, the three sets of precepts are, "I vow to put an end to all evils. I vow to cultivate all virtues. And I vow to liberate all beings." But now you say they're only for controlling the three poisoned states of mind. Isn't this contrary to the meaning of the scriptures?

佛所說是眞實語。菩薩摩訶薩。於過去因中修行時。爲對三毒。發三誓願。持一切淨戒。對於貪毒。誓斷一切惡。常修定。對於瞋毒。誓修一切善。常修慧。對於癡毒。度一切衆生。由持如是戒定慧等三種淨法。故能超彼三毒成佛道也。以能制三毒。則諸惡消滅。名爲斷。以能持三聚淨戒。則諸善具足。名之爲修。以能斷惡修善。則萬行成就。自它俱利。普濟群生。故名解脫。則知所修戒行不離於心。若自心淸淨。則一切佛土皆悉淸淨。故經云。心垢則衆生垢。心淨則衆生淨。欲得佛土。當淨其心。隨其心淨。則佛土淨也。故能制毒則三聚淨戒自然成就。

問曰。如經所說。六波羅蜜者。亦名六度。所謂布施持戒

The sutras of the Buddha are true. But long ago, when that great bodhisattva was cultivating the seed of enlightenment, it was to counter the three poisons that he made his three vows. Practicing moral prohibitions to counter the poison of greed, he vowed to put an end to all evils. Practicing meditation to counter the poison of anger, he vowed to cultivate all virtues. And practicing wisdom to counter the poison of delusion, he vowed to liberate all beings. Because he persevered in these three pure practices of morality, meditation, and wisdom, he was able to overcome the three poisons and reach enlightenment. By overcoming the three poisons he wiped out everything sinful and thus put an end to evil. By observing the three sets of precepts he did nothing but good and thus cultivated virtue. And by putting an end to evil and cultivating virtue he consummated all practices, benefited himself as well as others, and rescued mortals everywhere. Thus he liberated beings.

You should realize that the practice you cultivate doesn't exist apart from your mind. If your mind is pure, all buddha-lands are pure. The sutras say, "If their minds are impure, beings are impure. If their minds are pure, beings are pure." And "To reach a buddha-land, purify your mind. As your mind becomes pure, buddha-lands become pure." Thus by overcoming the three poisoned states of mind the three sets of precepts are automatically fulfilled.

But the sutras say the six paramitas are charity, morality,

忍辱精進禪定智慧。今言六根淸淨。名波羅蜜者。若爲通會。又六度者。其義如何。答。欲修六度。當淨六根。先降六賊。能捨眼賊。離諸色境。名爲布施。能禁耳賊。於彼聲塵。不令縱逸。名爲持戒。能伏鼻賊。等諸香臭。自在調柔。名爲忍辱。能制口賊。不貪諸味。讚詠講說。名爲精進。能降身賊。於諸觸欲。湛然不動。名爲禪定。能調意賊。不順無明。常修覺慧。名爲智慧。六度者運也。六波羅蜜。喻若船筏。能運衆生。達於彼岸。故名六度。

問。經云。釋迦如來。爲菩薩時。曾飲三斗六升乳糜。方成佛道。先因飲乳。後證佛果。豈唯觀心得解脫也。答。成佛如此。言無虛妄也。必因食乳。然始成佛。言食乳者。有二

patience, devotion, meditation, and wisdom. Now you say the paramitas refer to the purification of the senses. What do you mean by this? And why are they called ferries?

Cultivating the paramitas means purifying the six senses by overcoming the six thieves. Casting out the thief of the eye by abandoning the visual world is charity. Keeping out the thief of the ear by not listening to sounds is morality. Humbling the thief of the nose by equating all smells as neutral is patience. Controlling the thief of the mouth by conquering desires to taste, praise, and explain is devotion. Quelling the thief of the body by remaining unmoved by sensations of touch is meditation. And taming the thief of the mind by not yielding to delusions but practicing wakefulness is wisdom. These six paramitas are transports. Like boats or rafts, they transport beings to the other shore. Hence they're called ferries.

But when Shakyamuni was a bodhisattva, he consumed three bowls of milk and six ladles of gruel[89] *prior to attaining enlightenment. If he had to drink milk before he could taste the fruit of buddhahood, how can merely beholding the mind result in liberation?*

What you say is true. That is how he attained enlightenment. He had to drink milk before he could become a buddha. But there are two kinds of milk. That which Shakyamuni drank wasn't

種。佛所食者。非是世間不淨之乳。乃是清淨法乳。三斗者。三聚淨戒。六升者。六波羅蜜。成佛道時。由食如是清淨法乳。方證佛果。若言如來食於世間和合不淨牛羶腥乳。豈不謗誤之甚。眞如者。自是金剛不壞。無漏法身。永離世間一切諸苦。豈須如是不淨之乳。以充飢渴。經所說。其牛不在高原。不在下濕。不食穀麥糠麩。不與特牛同群。其牛身作紫磨金色。言牛者。毗盧舍那佛也。以大慈悲。憐愍一切。故於清淨法體中。出如是三聚淨戒六波羅蜜微妙法乳。養育一切求解脫者。如是眞淨之牛清淨之乳。非但如來飮之成道。一切衆生若能飮者。皆得阿耨多羅三藐三菩提。

ordinary impure milk but pure dharma-milk. The three bowls were the three sets of precepts. And the six ladles were the six paramitas. When Shakyamuni attained enlightenment, it was because he drank this pure dharma-milk that he tasted the fruit of buddhahood. To say that the Tathagata drank the worldly concoction of impure, rank-smelling cow's milk is the height of slander. That which is truly so, the indestructible, passionless dharma-self, remains forever free of the world's afflictions. Why would it need impure milk to satisfy its hunger or thirst?

The sutras say, "This ox doesn't live in the highlands or the lowlands. It doesn't eat grain or chaff. And it doesn't graze with cows. The body of this ox is the color of burnished gold." The ox refers to Vairocana.[90] Owing to his great compassion for all beings, he produces from within his pure dharma-body the sublime dharma-milk of the three sets of precepts and six paramitas to nourish all those who seek liberation. The pure milk of such a truly pure ox not only enabled the Tathagata to achieve buddhahood but also enables any being who drinks it to attain unexcelled, complete enlightenment.

問。經中所說。佛令眾生修造伽藍。鑄寫形像。燒香散花、然燈。晝夜六時遶塔行道。持齋禮拜。種種功德。皆成佛道。若唯觀心。總攝諸行。說如是事。應虛空也。答。佛所說經。有無量方便。以一切眾生。鈍根狹劣。不悟甚深之義、所以假有為。喻無為。若復不修內行。唯只外求。希望獲福。無有是處。言伽藍者。西國梵語。此土翻為清淨地也、若永除三毒。常淨六根。身心湛然。內外清淨。是名修伽藍。鑄寫形像者。即是一切眾生求佛道也。所為修諸覺行。彷像如來真容妙相。豈遣鑄寫金銅之所作也。是故求解脫者。以身為爐。以法為火。以智慧為巧匠。三聚淨戒。六波羅蜜。以為模樣。鎔鍊身中真如佛性。遍入一切

Throughout the sutras the Buddha tells mortals they can achieve enlightenment by performing such meritorious works as building monasteries, casting statues, burning incense, scattering flowers, lighting eternal lamps, practicing all six periods[91] *of the day and night, walking around stupas,*[92] *observing fasts, and worshipping. But if beholding the mind includes all other practices, then such works as these would appear redundant.*

The sutras of the Buddha contain countless metaphors. Because mortals have shallow minds and don't understand anything deep, the Buddha used the tangible to represent the sublime. People who seek blessings by concentrating on external works instead of internal cultivation are attempting the impossible.

What you call a monastery we call a *sangharama*, a place of purity. But whoever denies entry to the three poisons and keeps the gates of his senses pure, his body and mind still, inside and outside clean, builds a monastery.

Casting statues refers to all practices cultivated by those who seek enlightenment. The Tathagata's sublime form can't be represented by metal. Those who seek enlightenment regard their bodies as the furnace, the Dharma as the fire, wisdom as the craftsmanship, and the three sets of precepts and six paramitas as the mold. They smelt and refine the true buddha-nature within themselves and

戒律模中。如教奉行。一無漏缺。自然成就眞容之像。所謂究竟常住微妙色身。非是有爲敗壞之法。若人求道。不解如是鑄寫眞容。憑何輒言功德。燒香者。亦非世間有相之香。乃是無爲正法之香也。薰諸臭穢無明惡業。悉令消滅。其正法香者。有其五種。一者戒香。所謂能斷諸惡。能修諸善。二者定香。所謂深信大乘。心無退轉。三者慧香。所謂常於身心。內外觀察。四者解脫香。所謂能斷一切無明結縛。五者解脫知見香。所謂觀照常明。通達無礙。如是五種香。名爲最上之香。世間無比。佛在世日。令諸弟子以智慧火。燒如是無價珍香。供養十方諸佛。今時衆生不解如來眞實之義。唯將外火燒世間沈

pour it into the mold formed by the rules of discipline. Acting in perfect accordance with the Buddha's teaching, they naturally create a perfect likeness. The eternal, sublime body isn't subject to conditions or decay. If you seek the Truth but don't learn how to make a true likeness, what will you use in its place?

And burning incense doesn't mean ordinary material incense but the incense of the intangible Dharma, which drives away filth, ignorance, and evil deeds with its perfume. There are five kinds of such dharma-incense.[93] First is the incense of morality, which means renouncing evil and cultivating virtue. Second is the incense of meditation, which means deeply believing in the Mahayana with unwavering resolve. Third is the incense of wisdom, which means contemplating the body and mind, inside and out. Fourth is the incense of liberation, which means severing the bonds of ignorance. And fifth is the incense of perfect knowledge, which means being always aware and nowhere obstructed. These five are the most precious kinds of incense and far superior to anything the world has to offer.

When the Buddha was in the world, he told his disciples to light such precious incense with the fire of awareness as an offering to the buddhas of the ten directions. But people today don't understand the Tathagata's real meaning. They use an ordinary flame to light material incense of sandalwood or frankincense and pray for some future blessing that never comes.

檀薰陸質礙之香。希望福報。云何得散花者。義亦如是。所謂常說正法。諸功德花。饒益有情。散沾一切。於眞如性。普施莊嚴。此功德花。佛所讚歎。究竟常住。無彫落期。若復有人散如是花。獲福無量。若言如來令衆生。剪截繒彩。傷損草木。以爲散花。無有是處。所以者何。持淨戒者。於諸天地。森羅萬像。不令觸犯。誤犯者。猶獲大罪。況復今者故毁淨戒。傷萬物求於福報。欲益返損。豈有是乎。又長明燈者。卽正覺心也。以覺明了。喻之爲燈。是故一切求解脫者。以身爲燈臺。心爲燈炷。增諸戒行。以爲添油。智慧明達。喻如燈火。當燃如是眞正覺燈。照破一切無明癡暗。能以此法。轉相開示。卽是一燈燃百千燈。

For scattering flowers the same holds true. This refers to speaking the Dharma, scattering flowers of virtue, in order to benefit others and glorify the real self. These flowers of virtue are those praised by the Buddha. They last forever and never fade. And whoever scatters such flowers reaps infinite blessings. If you think the Tathagata meant for people to harm plants by cutting off their flowers, you're wrong. Those who observe the precepts don't injure any of the myriad life forms of heaven and earth. If you hurt something by mistake, you suffer for it. But those who intentionally break the precepts by injuring the living for the sake of future blessings suffer even more. How could they let would-be blessings turn into sorrows?

The eternal lamp represents perfect awareness. Likening the illumination of awareness to that of a lamp, those who seek liberation see their body as the lamp, their mind as its wick, the addition of discipline as its oil, and the power of wisdom as its flame. By lighting this lamp of perfect awareness they dispel all darkness and delusion. And by passing this dharma on to others they're able to use one lamp to light thousands of lamps. And because these lamps likewise light countless other lamps, their light lasts forever.

以燈續然。然燈無盡。故號長明。過去有佛。名曰然燈。義亦如是。愚癡衆生。不會如來方便之說。專行虛妄。執著有爲。遂燃世間蘇油之燈。以照空室。乃稱依教。豈不謬乎。所以者何。佛放眉間一毫相光。上能照萬八千世界。豈假如是蘇油之燈。以爲利益。審察斯理。應不然乎。又六時行道者。所謂六根之中。於一切時。常行佛道。修諸覺行。調伏六根。長時不捨。名爲六時。遶塔行道者。塔是身心也。當令覺慧巡遶身心。念念不停。名爲遶塔。過去諸聖。皆行此道。得至涅槃。今時世人。不會此理。曾不內行。唯執外求。將質礙身。遶世間塔。日夜走驟。徒自疲勞。而於眞性。一無利益。又持齋者。當須會意。不達斯理。徒

Long ago, there was a buddha named Dipamkara,[94] or *Lamp-lighter*. This was the meaning of his name. But fools don't understand the metaphors of the Tathagata. Persisting in delusions and clinging to the tangible, they light lamps of everyday vegetable oil and think that by illuminating the interiors of buildings they're following the Buddha's teaching. How foolish! The light released by a buddha from one curl[95] between his brows can illuminate countless worlds. An oil lamp is no help. Or do you think otherwise?

Practicing all six periods of the day and night means constantly cultivating enlightenment among the six senses and persevering in every form of awareness. Never relaxing control over the six senses is what's meant by all six periods.

As for walking around stupas, the stupa is your body and mind. When your awareness circles your body and mind without stopping, this is called walking around a stupa. The sages of long ago followed this path to nirvana. But people today don't understand what this means. Instead of looking inside they insist on looking outside. They use their material bodies to walk around material stupas. And they keep at it day and night, wearing themselves out in vain and coming no closer to their real self.

The same holds true for observing a fast. It's useless unless you understand what this really means. To fast means to regulate,

爾虛切。齋者齊也。所謂齋正身心。不令散亂。持者護也。所謂於諸戒行。如法護持。必須外禁六情。內制三毒。勤覺察淨身心。了如是義。名爲持齋。又持齋者。食有五種。一者法喜食。所謂依持正法。歡喜奉行。二者禪悅食。所謂內外澄寂。身心悅樂。三者念食。所謂常念諸佛。心口相應。四者願食。所謂行住坐臥。常求善願。五者解脫食。所謂心常清淨。不染俗塵。此五種食。名爲齋食。若復有人。不食如是五種淨食。自言持齋。無有是處。唯斷於無明之食。若輒觸者。名爲破齋。若有破。云何獲福。世有迷人。不悟斯理。身心放逸。諸惡皆爲。貪慾恣情。不生慚愧。唯斷外食。自爲持齋。必無是事。又禮拜者。當如是法也。

to regulate your body and mind so that they're not distracted or disturbed. And to observe means to uphold, to uphold the rules of discipline according to the Dharma. Fasting means guarding against the six attractions[96] on the outside and the three poisons on the inside and striving through contemplation to purify your body and mind.

Fasting also includes five kinds of food. First there's delight in the Dharma. This is the delight that comes from acting in accordance with the Dharma. Second is harmony in meditation. This is the harmony of body and mind that comes from seeing through subject and object. Third is invocation, the invocation of buddhas with both your mouth and your mind. Fourth is resolution, the resolution to pursue virtue whether walking, standing, sitting, or lying down. And fifth is liberation, the liberation of your mind from worldly contamination. These five are the foods of fasting. Unless a person eats these five pure foods, he's wrong to think he's fasting.

Also, once you stop eating the food of delusion, if you touch it again you break your fast. And once you break it, you reap no blessing from it. The world is full of deluded people who don't see this. They indulge their body and mind in all manner of evil. They give free rein to their passions and have no shame. And when they stop eating ordinary food, they call it fasting. How absurd!

It's the same with worshipping. You have to understand the

必須理體內明。事隨權變。理有行藏。會如是義。乃名依法。夫禮者敬也。拜者伏也。所謂恭敬眞性。屈伏無明。名爲禮拜。若能惡情永滅。善念恒存。雖不現相。名爲禮拜。其相卽法相也。世尊欲令世俗表謙下心。亦爲禮拜。故須屈伏外身。示內恭敬。舉外明內。性相相應。若復不行理法。唯執外求。內則放縱瞋癡。常爲惡業。外卽空勞身相。詐現威儀。無慚於聖。徒誑於凡。不免輪迴。豈成功德。問如温室經說。洗浴衆僧。獲福無量。此則憑於事法。功德始成。若爲觀心可相應否。答洗浴衆僧者。非洗世間有爲事也。世尊當爾爲諸弟子說温室經。欲令受持洗浴之法。故假世事。比喻眞宗。隱說七事供養功德。其七

meaning and adapt to conditions. Meaning includes action and nonaction. Whoever understands this follows the Dharma.

Worship means reverence and humility. It means revering your real self and humbling delusions. If you can wipe out evil desires and harbor good thoughts, even if nothing shows, it's worship. Such form is its real form.

The Lord[97] wanted worldly people to think of worship as expressing humility and subduing the mind. So he told them to prostrate their bodies to show their reverence, to let the external express the internal, to harmonize essence and form. Those who fail to cultivate the inner meaning and concentrate instead on the outward expression never stop indulging in ignorance, hatred, and evil while exhausting themselves to no avail. They can deceive others with postures, remain shameless before sages and vain before mortals, but they'll never escape the Wheel, much less achieve any merit.

But the Bathhouse Sutra[98] *says, "By contributing to the bathing of monks, people receive limitless blessings." This would appear to be an instance of external practice achieving merit. How does this relate to beholding the mind?*

Here, the bathing of monks doesn't refer to the washing of anything tangible. When the Lord preached the *Bathhouse Sutra*, he wanted his disciples to remember the dharma of washing. So he used an everyday concern to convey his real meaning, which he couched in his explanation of merit from seven offerings. Of these

事云何。一者淨水。二者燒火。三者澡豆。四者楊枝。五者淨灰。六者蘇膏。七者內衣。以此七法喻於七事。一切衆生由此七法沐浴莊嚴。能除毒心無明垢穢。其七法者。一者謂淨戒。洗蕩僭非。猶如淨水濯諸塵垢。二者智慧觀察內外。猶如然火。能溫淨水。三者分別簡棄諸惡。猶如澡豆能淨垢膩。四者眞實斷諸妄想。如嚼楊枝能淨口氣。五者正信決定無疑。猶如淨灰摩身。能辟諸風。六者謂柔和忍辱。猶如蘇膏通潤皮膚。七者謂慚愧悔諸惡業。猶如內衣遮醜形體。如上七法。是經中秘密之義如來當爾爲諸大乘利根者說。非爲小智下劣凡夫。所以今人無能解悟。其溫室者。卽身是也。所以燃智慧火。

seven, the first is clear water, the second fire, the third soap, the fourth willow catkins, the fifth pure ashes, the sixth ointment, and the seventh the inner garment.[99] He used these seven to represent seven other things that cleanse and enhance a person by eliminating the delusion and filth of a poisoned mind.

The first of these seven is morality, which washes away excess just as clear water washes away dirt. Second is wisdom, which penetrates subject and object, just as fire warms water. Third is discrimination, which gets rid of evil practices, just as soap gets rid of grime. Fourth is honesty, which purges delusions, just as chewing willow catkins purifies the breath. Fifth is true faith, which resolves all doubts, just as rubbing pure ashes on the body prevents illnesses. Sixth is patience, which overcomes resistance and disgrace, just as ointment softens the skin. And seventh is shame, which redresses evil deeds, just as the inner garment covers up an ugly body. These seven represent the real meaning of the sutra. When he spoke this sutra, the Tathagata was talking to farsighted followers of the Mahayana, not to narrow-minded people of dim vision. It's not surprising that people nowadays don't understand.

The bathhouse is the body. When you light the fire of wisdom,

温淨戒湯沐浴身中。眞如佛性。受持七法。以自莊嚴。當爾比丘。聰明上智。皆悟聖意。如說修行。功德成就。俱登聖果。今時衆生。莫測其事。將世間水。洗質礙身。自謂依經。豈非誤也。且眞如佛性。非是凡形。煩惱塵垢。本來無相。豈可將質礙水。洗無爲身。事不相應。云何悟道。若欲身得淨者。當觀此身。本因貪欲。不淨所生。臭穢駢闐。內外充滿。若也洗此身求於淨者。猶如塹塹盡方淨。以此驗之。明知洗外非佛說也。

問經說言至心念佛。必得往生西方淨土。以此一門。即應成佛。何假觀心。求於解脫。答。夫念佛者。當須正念。了義爲正。不了義爲邪。正念必得往生。邪念云何達彼。佛

you warm the pure water of the precepts and bathe the true buddha-nature within you. By upholding these seven practices you add to your virtue. The monks of that age were perceptive. They understood the Buddha's meaning. They followed his teaching, perfected their virtue, and tasted the fruit of buddhahood. But people nowadays can't fathom these things. They use ordinary water to wash a physical body and think they're following the sutra. But they're mistaken.

Our true buddha-nature has no shape. And the dust of affliction has no form. How can people use ordinary water to wash an intangible body? It won't work. When will they wake up? To clean such a body you have to behold it. Once impurities and filth arise from desire, they multiply until they cover you inside and out. But if you try to wash this body of yours, you'll have to scrub until it's nearly gone before it's clean. From this you should realize that washing something external isn't what the Buddha meant.

The sutras say that someone who wholeheartedly invokes the Buddha is sure to be reborn in the Western Paradise.[100] *Since this door leads to buddhahood, why seek liberation in beholding the mind?*

If you're going to invoke the Buddha, you have to do it right. Unless you understand what invoking means, you'll do it wrong. And if you do it wrong, you'll never go anywhere.

者覺也所謂覺察身心勿令起惡念者憶也所謂憶持戒行不忘精進勤了如是義名爲念故知念在於心不在於言因筌求魚得魚忘筌因言求意得意忘言既稱念佛之名須知念佛之道若心無實口誦空名三毒內臻人我塡臆將無明心不見佛徒爾費功且如誦之與念義理懸殊在口曰誦在心曰念故知念從心起名爲覺行之門誦在口中卽是音聲之相執相求理終無是處故知過去諸聖所修皆非外說唯只推心卽心是衆善之源卽心爲萬德之主涅槃常樂由息心生三界輪迴亦從心起心是一世之門戶心是解脫之關津知門戶者豈慮難成知關津者何憂不達竊見今時淺識唯

Buddha means awareness, the awareness of body and mind that prevents evil from arising in either. And to invoke means to call to mind, to call constantly to mind the rules of discipline and to follow them with all your might. This is what's meant by invoking. Invoking has to do with thought and not with language. If you use a trap to catch fish, once you succeed you can forget the trap. And if you use language to find meaning, once you find it you can forget language.

To invoke the Buddha's name you have to understand the dharma of invoking. If it's not present in your mind, your mouth chants an empty name. As long as you're troubled by the three poisons or by thoughts of yourself, your deluded mind will keep you from seeing the Buddha and you'll only waste your effort. Chanting and invoking are worlds apart. Chanting is done with the mouth. Invoking is done with the mind. And because invoking comes from the mind, it's called the door to awareness. Chanting is centered in the mouth and appears as sound. If you cling to appearances while searching for meaning, you won't find a thing. Thus, sages of the past cultivated introspection and not speech.

This mind is the source of all virtues. And this mind is the chief of all powers. The eternal bliss of nirvana comes from the mind at rest. Rebirth in the three realms also comes from the mind. The mind is the door to every world and the mind is the ford to the other shore. Those who know where the door is don't worry about reaching it. Those who know where the ford is don't worry about crossing it.

The people I meet nowadays are superficial. They think of

知事相爲功。廣費財寶。多傷水陸。妄營像塔。虛促人夫。積木疊泥。圖靑畫綠。傾心盡力。損己迷他。未解慚愧。何曾覺知見有爲則勤勤愛著。說無相則兀兀如迷。且貪現世之小慈。豈覺當來之大苦。此之修學。徒自疲勞。背正歸邪。誑言獲福。但能攝心內照。覺觀外明。絕三毒永使銷亡。閉六賊不令侵擾。自然恒沙功德。種種莊嚴。無數法門。一一成就。超凡證聖。目擊非遙。悟在須臾。何煩皓首。眞門幽秘。寧可具陳。略述觀心。詳其少分。

達磨大師破相論終

merit as something that has form. They squander their wealth and butcher creatures of land and sea. They foolishly concern themselves with erecting statues and stupas, telling people to pile up lumber and bricks, to paint this blue and that green. They strain body and mind, injure themselves and mislead others. And they don't know enough to be ashamed. How will they ever become enlightened? They see something tangible and instantly become attached. If you talk to them about formlessness, they sit there dumb and confused. Greedy for the small mercies of this world, they remain blind to the great suffering to come. Such disciples wear themselves out in vain. Turning from the true to the false, they talk about nothing but future blessings.

If you can simply concentrate your mind's inner light and behold its outer illumination, you'll dispel the three poisons and drive away the six thieves once and for all. And without effort you'll gain possession of an infinite number of virtues, perfections, and doors to the truth. Seeing through the mundane and witnessing the sublime is less than an eye-blink away. Realization is now. Why worry about gray hair? But the true door is hidden and can't be revealed. I have only touched upon beholding the mind.

NOTES

The Chinese text used for this translation is a Ch'ing dynasty woodblock edition that incorporates corrections of obvious copyist errors in the standard edition of the continuation to the Ming dynasty Tripitaka. I've added several corrections of my own, based mostly on textual variants found in Tunhuang versions, for which see D. T. Suzuki's *Shoshitsu isho oyobi kaisetsu* (Lost Works of Bodhidharma). An earlier English translation of the *Outline of Practice* (from the *Transmission of the Lamp*) appears in Suzuki's *Manual of Zen Buddhism*. Also, in *Zen Dawn* J. C. Cleary has recently published translations based on Tunhuang editions of the *Outline* (from the *Records of Masters and Students of the Lanka*) and the *Breakthrough Sermon* (On Contemplating Mind).

1. *Path*. When Buddhism came to China, *Tao* was used to translate *Dharma* and *Bodhi*. This was partly because Buddhism was viewed as a foreign version of Taoism. In his "Bloodstream Sermon," Bodhidharma says, "The path is zen."
2. *Walls*. After he arrived in China, Bodhidharma spent nine years in meditation facing the rock wall of a cave near Shaolin Temple. Bodhidharma's walls of emptiness connect all opposites, including self and other, mortal and sage.
3. *Four . . . practices*. These are a variation of the Four Noble Truths: all existence is marked by suffering; suffering has a cause; the cause can be brought to an end; and the way to bring it to an end is the Eightfold Noble Path of right views, right thought, right speech, right action, right livelihood, right devotion, right mindfulness, and right zen.
4. *Calamity . . . Prosperity*. Two goddesses, responsible for bad and good fortune, respectively. They appear in Chapter Twelve of the *Nirvana Sutra*.
5. *Three realms*. The Buddhist psychological equivalent of the Brahmanic cosmological triple world of *bhur*, *bhuvah*, and *svar*, or *earth*, *atmosphere*, and *heaven*. The Buddhist triple world includes *kamadhatu*, or the realm of desire—the hells, the four continents of the human and animal world, and the six heavens of pleasure; *rupadhatu*, or the realm of form—the four heavens of meditation; and *arupad-*

hatu, or the formless realm of pure spirit—the four empty, or immaterial, states. Together, the three realms constitute the limits of existence. In Chapter Three of the *Lotus Sutra* the three realms are represented by a burning house.

6. *Dharma*. The Sanskrit word *dharma* comes from *dhri*, meaning *to hold*, and refers to anything held to be real, whether in a provisional or in an ultimate sense. Hence, the word can mean *thing*, *teaching*, or *reality*.
7. *Six virtues*. The paramitas, or *means to the other shore*: charity, morality, patience, devotion, meditation, and wisdom. All six must be practiced with detachment from the concepts of actor, action, and beneficiary.
8. *Mind*. A verse from the *Avatamsaka Sutra* is paraphrased here: "The three realms are just one mind." The sixth Zen patriarch, Hui-neng, distinguishes *mind* as the realm and *nature* as the lord.
9. *Buddhas*. Buddhism doesn't limit itself to one buddha. It recognizes countless buddhas. After all, everyone has the buddha-nature. There's a buddha in every world, just as there's awareness in every thought. The only necessary qualification for buddhahood is complete awareness.
10. *Without . . . definitions*. The absence of definitions in the transmission of the Dharma is a touchstone of Zen Buddhism. It doesn't necessarily mean without words but, rather, without restrictions as to the mode of transmission. A gesture is as good as a discourse.
11. *Kalpa*. The period from a world's creation until its destruction; an aeon.
12. *This mind is the buddha*. This is Mahayana Buddhism in a nutshell. Once a monk asked Big Plum what Matsu taught him. Big Plum said, "This mind is the buddha." The monk replied, "Nowadays Matsu teaches *That which isn't the mind isn't the buddha*." To this Big Plum responded, "Let him have *That which isn't the mind isn't the buddha*. I'll stick with *This mind is the buddha*." When he heard this story, Matsu said, "The plum is ripe." (*Transmission of the Lamp*, Chapter 7)
13. *Enlightenment*. Bodhi. The mind free of delusion is said to be full of light, like the moon when it's no longer obscured by clouds. Instead of undergoing another rebirth, the enlightened person attains nirvana, because enlightenment puts an end to karma. The faculty of hearing

is more primitive, but sight is man's accustomed source of knowledge about reality; hence the use of visual metaphors. The sutras, though, also talk about worlds in which buddhas teach through the sense of smell.

14. *Nirvana.* Early Chinese translators tried some forty Chinese words before finally giving up and simply transliterating this Sanskrit word, which means *absence of breath*. It's also defined as *the only calm*. Most people equate it with death, but to Buddhists nirvana means the absence of the dialectic that breath represents. According to Nagarjuna, "That which is, when subject to karma, samsara, is, when no longer subject to karma, nirvana." (*Madhyamika Shastra*, Chapter 25, Verse 9)

15. *Self-nature.* Svabhava. That which is of itself so. Self-nature depends on nothing, either causally, temporally, or spatially. Self-nature has no appearance. Its body is no body. It's not some sort of ego, and it's not some sort of substrate or characteristic that exists in or apart from phenomena. Self-nature is empty of all characteristics, including emptiness, and yet it defines reality.

16. *Invoke a buddha.* Invocation includes both visualization of a buddha and repetition of a buddha's name. The usual object of such devotion is Amitabha, the Buddha of the Infinite. Wholehearted invocation of Amitabha assures devotees of rebirth in his Western Paradise, where enlightenment is said to be far easier to attain than in this world.

17. *Sutra.* Meaning *string*, a sutra strings together the words of a buddha.

18. *Precepts.* The Buddhist practice of morality includes a number of prohibitions: usually 5 for laymen, nearly 250 for monks, and anywhere from 350 to 500 for nuns.

19. *See your nature.* Whether called *self-nature*, *buddha-nature*, or *dharma-nature*, our nature is our real body. It's also our false body. Our real body isn't subject to birth or death, appearance or disappearance, but our false body is in a state of constant change. Seeing our nature, our nature sees itself, because delusion and awareness aren't different. For an exposition of this in English, see D. T. Suzuki's *Zen Doctrine of No Mind*.

20. *Life and death.* Shakyamuni left home to find a way out of the endless round of life and death. Anyone who follows the Buddha must do the same. When it was time to transmit the robe and bowl of the Zen lineage, Hung-jen, the fifth Zen patriarch, called his disciples together

and told them, "Nothing is more important than life and death. But instead of looking for a way out of the Sea of Life and Death, you spend all your time looking for ways to earn merit. If you're blind to your own nature, what good is merit? Use your wisdom, the prajna-nature of your own mind. All of you, go write me a poem." (*Sutra of the Sixth Patriarch*, Chapter One)

21. *Twelvefold Canon*. The twelve divisions of the scriptures recognized by Mahayana Buddhism. These divisions, which were made to separate different subjects and literary forms, include *sutras*, sermons of the Buddha; *geyas*, verse repetitions of sutras; *gathas*, chants and poems; *nidanas*, historical narratives; *jatakas*, stories of previous buddhas; *itivrittakas*, stories of past lives of disciples; *adbhuta-dharma*, miracles of the Buddha; *avadana*, allegories; *upadesa*, discussions of doctrine; *udana*, unsolicited statements of doctrine; *vaipulya*, extended discourses; and *vyakarana*, prophecies of enlightenment.
22. *The Wheel of Birth and Death*. The endless round of rebirth from which only buddhas escape.
23. *Good Star*. In Chapter Thirty-three of the *Nirvana Sutra*, Good Star is said to be one of Shakyamuni's three sons. And, like his brother Rahula, he became a monk. Eventually, he was able to recite and explain the entire sacred literature of his time and thought he had attained nirvana. In fact, he had only reached the fourth dhyana heaven in the realm of form. And when the karmic support for such attainment ran out, he was transported bodily to the hell of endless suffering.
24. *Sutras or shastras*. Sutras are the discourses of buddhas. Shastras are the discourses of prominent disciples.
25. *White from black*. A reference to the attempt to see Buddhism as Confucianism or Taoism, sparked by Hui-lin's essay on the subject written in 435, in which he called Confucianism and Buddhism equally true and in which he denied the operation of karma after death.
26. *Devils*. Buddhists, like the followers of other faiths, recognize a category of being whose sole purpose is to sidetrack would-be buddhas. These legions of devils are led by Mara, whom the Buddha defeated the night of his enlightenment.
27. *Karma*. The moral equivalent of the physical law of cause and effect, karma includes actions of the body, mouth, and mind. All such actions turn the Wheel of Rebirth and result in suffering. Even when an action is good, it still turns the Wheel. The goal of Buddhist practice

is to escape the Wheel, to put an end to karma, to act without acting, not to achieve a better rebirth.

28. *Skandhas*. Sanskrit for the constituents of mind or one's mental body: form, sensation, perception, impulse, and consciousness.

29. *Samsara*. Sanskrit for *constant flow*, the round of mortality, the endless flux of birth and death.

30. *Tathagata*. A name for a buddha; the name by which a buddha refers to himself. A buddha is aware. A tathagata is a buddha's manifestation in the world, his transformation body, as opposed to his reward body or his real body. A tathagata teaches the Dharma.

31. *Four elements*. The four constituents of all matter, including the material body: earth, water, fire, and air.

32. *Kashyapa*. Also called Mahakashyapa, or the Great Kashyapa. He was one of the Buddha's foremost disciples and is credited with becoming the first Zen patriarch in India. When the Buddha held up a flower, Kashyapa smiled in response, and the transmission of the zen mind began.

33. *Bodhisattva*. The Mahayana ideal. The bodhisattva ties his own liberation to that of other beings, whereas the arhat, the Hinayana ideal, concerns himself with seeking his own salvation. Instead of shrinking the mind into nothingness, as the arhat does, the bodhisattva expands it to infinity. This is because he realizes that all beings have the same buddha-nature.

34. *Spirits, demons, or divine beings*. Spirits are disembodied beings. Demons include various gods of the sky (*devas*), the sea (*nagas*), and the earth (*yakshas*). Divine beings include Indra, lord of the thirty-three heavens, and Brahma, lord of creation.

35. *A buddha, a dharma, or a bodhisattva*. These three constitute the Buddhist Refuge, or Triple Jewel. A dharma is the teaching of a buddha. Those who follow such a teaching constitute the order of monks or, in the Mahayana tradition, bodhisattvas.

36. *Zen*. First used to transliterate *dhyana*, the Sanskrit term for meditation. Bodhidharma is credited with freeing zen from the meditation cushion, using the term instead in reference to the everyday, straightforward mind, the mind that sits without sitting and that acts without acting.

37. *Thousands of sutras and shastras*. A catalogue of the Chinese Buddhist Canon, or Tripitaka, made in the early sixth century lists 2,213 distinct works, about 1,600 of which were sutras. Many sutras have

been added to the Tripitaka since then, but even more have been lost. The present Canon includes 1,662 works.

38. *Body and mind.* The body of four elements and the mind of five aggregates designate the self generally, but Bodhidharma is referring to the buddha-self.

39. *Heaven and hell.* Buddhists recognize four heavens of form, which are divided into sixteen to eighteen heavens, and four of formlessness. At the opposite side of the Wheel are eight hot hells and eight cold hells, each of which has four adjacent hells. There are also a number of special hells, such as the hells of endless darkness and endless suffering.

40. *Fanatics.* Among the followers of various Buddhist and non-Buddhist religious sects, those most subject to denigration as fanatics were those who engaged in asceticism and self-torture or who followed the letter and not the spirit of the Dharma.

41. *Unexcelled, complete enlightenment.* Anuttara-samyak-sambodhi. The goal of bodhisattvas. See the beginning of the *Diamond Sutra.*

42. *Shakyamuni.* Shakya was the Buddha's clan name. *Muni* means saint. His family name was Gautama, and his personal name was Siddhartha. The exact dates given for him vary, but the consensus is from 557 to 487 B.C. or thereabouts.

43. *Ananda.* Shakyamuni's brother-in-law. He was born the night of the Buddha's Enlightenment. Twenty-five years later he entered the Order as the Buddha's personal attendant. After the Buddha's Nirvana, he repeated from memory the Buddha's sermons at the First Council.

44. *Arhat.* To free oneself from rebirth is the goal of followers of the Hinayana, or Small Vehicle. But while an arhat is beyond passion, he's also beyond compassion. He doesn't realize that all mortals share the same nature and that there aren't any buddhas unless everyone's a buddha.

45. *Icchantikas.* A class of being concerned so exclusively with sensual gratification that religious belief is beyond them. They break the precepts and refuse to repent. An early Chinese translation of the *Nirvana Sutra* denied that icchantikas possessed the buddha-nature. Since the Buddhist prohibition against killing is intended to prevent killing anyone capable of buddhahood, killing icchantikas was, at least in theory, held to be blameless. A later translation of the *Nirvana Sutra,* however, rectified this notion, asserting that even icchantikas have the buddha-nature.

46. *Lower orders of existence.* Beasts, hungry ghosts, and sufferers in hell.

47. *Shave their heads.* When Shakyamuni left his father's palace in the middle of the night to begin his search for enlightenment, he cut off his shoulder-length hair with his sword. The short hair that remained formed clockwise curls that never required cutting again. Later, members of the Buddhist Order began shaving their heads to distinguish themselves from other sects.

48. *Spiritual powers.* Buddhists recognize six such powers: the ability to see all forms; the ability to hear all sounds; the ability to know the thoughts of others; the ability to know the previous existences of oneself and others; the ability to be anywhere or do anything at will; and the ability to know the end of rebirth.

49. *Twenty-seven patriarchs.* Kashyapa was the first patriarch of the Zen lineage. Ananda was the second. Prajnatara was the twenty-seventh and Bodhidharma the twenty-eighth. Bodhidharma was also the first Zen patriarch in China.

50. *Imprint.* An imprint because transmission of the zen mind leaves a perfect likeness, which can always be checked against the real thing, and which takes as much time and makes as much sound as affixing a seal.

51. *Mahayana. Maha* means *great*, and *yana* means *vehicle*. The predominant form of Buddhism in Northern, Central, and East Asia. The Theravada (Teaching of the Elders) is the predominant form in South and Southeast Asia. The term *Hinayana* is also used to refer to the Theravada.

52. *Atoms.* The early Buddhist Sarvastivadins recognized subatomic particles called *parama-anu* which can only be known through meditation. Seven of these particles make up an atom, and seven atoms make up a molecule, which is perceptible only by the eyes of a bodhisattva. The Sarvastivadins claimed that a person's body is made up of 84,000 such atoms (the number 84,000 was often used to mean countless).

53. *Great Vehicle.* The Mahayana. The mind. Only the mind can take you everywhere.

54. *Six senses.* Sight, hearing, smell, taste, touch, and thought.

55. *Five aggregates.* The five skandhas, or constituents of mind: form, sensation, perception, impulse, and consciousness.

56. *Ten directions.* The eight points of the compass, plus the zenith and nadir.

57. *Arhats stay still.* The arhat achieves the fourth and final fruit of Hinayana Buddhists, freedom from passion, by cultivating stillness.

58. *Leaving home*. As Shakyamuni did to seek enlightenment. Hence, becoming a monk or nun.
59. *Place of enlightenment*. Bodhimandala. The center of every world, where all buddhas reach enlightenment. The term also refers to a Buddhist temple.
60. *Uninhabited place*. One suitable for spiritual cultivation.
61. *Middle Way*. The path that avoids realism and nihilism, existence and nonexistence.
62. *True vision*. The Buddha's Eightfold Noble Path begins with true vision, which is intended to break through delusion or ignorance, the first of twelve links on the Chain of Karma: delusion, impulse, consciousness, name-and-form, sense organs, contact, sensation, desire, grasping, existence, birth, aging-and-death. The first two refer to the previous existence, the last two to the next.
63. *Samadhi*. The goal of meditation. *Samadhi* is Sanskrit for an undistracted mind, a snake in a bamboo tube.
64. *Five shades*. The skandhas or aggregates, the constituents of personality that overshadow the real self: form, sensation, perception, impulse, and consciousness.
65. *Beginning of nirvana*. Nirvana isn't final until the body is left behind.
66. *Assurance of no rebirth*. The embodiment of nirvana.
67. *Buddha-land*. A realm transformed by the presence of a buddha from filth to purity: hence, a pure land. See the last section of Chapter One in the *Vimilakirti Sutra*.
68. *Raft*. The Buddha likens his teachings to a raft that can be used to cross the River of Endless Rebirth. But once it's served its purpose, the raft is useless. It's no longer a raft.
69. *Goddess . . . stable boy*. The goddess appears in Chapter Seven of the *Vimilakirti Sutra*. The stable boy may be a reference to Chandaka, Shakyamuni's groom. If it is, I'm not familiar with the story.
70. *Twelve entrances*. The six organs and the six senses.
71. *Three releases*. Release from delusion, anger, and greed lies through the three doors to deliverance: no-self, no-form, and no-desire.
72. *Wutou and futzu*. An anesthetic is extracted from futzu, the secondary roots that grow from the base root of wutou (*Aconitum* or monkshood). The secondary roots don't develop until the plant's second year.
73. *Three bodies*. The *nirmanakaya* (Shakyamuni), the *sambhogakaya* (Amitabha), and the *dharmakaya* (Vairocana).

74. *The Great Enlightenment occurred in the Himalayas.* The Buddha's Enlightenment occurred not in the Himalayas but in the ancient Indian state of Magadha, south of Nepal. In a previous existence, however, the Buddha lived in the Himalayas as an ascetic. Hence by linking together the Buddha's previous lives the claim is true.

75. *A person can enlarge the Way. The Way can't enlarge a person.* A statement by Confucius. (*Analects*, Chapter 15)

76. *Perfect wisdom.* This is a paraphrase of the opening line of the *Heart Sutra*, where the bodhisattva is Avalokitesvara and where perfect wisdom, or *prajnaparamita*, is no wisdom, because perfect wisdom is "gone, gone beyond, gone completely beyond" categories of space and time, being and nonbeing.

77. *Pure and impure.* For an extended discourse on these, see Ashvaghosa's *Awakening of Faith in the Mahayana*, where *pure* and *impure* are called *enlightenment* and *nonenlightenment*.

78. *Sutra of Ten Stages . . . Nirvana Sutra.* When translations of these two sutras first appeared in the early fifth century, they had a profound effect on the development of Buddhism in China. Among their teachings are the universality of the buddha-nature and the eternal, joyous, personal, and pure nature of nirvana. Up until then, the doctrine of emptiness taught by the *prajnaparamita* sutras had dominated Chinese Buddhism. The *Sutra of Ten Stages*, which details the stages through which a bodhisattva passes on his way to buddhahood, is a version of a chapter by the same title in the *Avatamsaka Sutra*.

79. *Six sense organs.* The eyes, ears, nose, tongue, skin, and mind.

80. *Six kinds of consciousness.* The varieties of consciousness associated with sight, hearing, smell, taste, touch, and thought. The *Lankavatara* breaks thought into comprehension, discrimination, and (tathagata-) memory for a total of eight forms of consciousness.

81. *Six states of existence.* The basic varieties of existence through which beings move, whether thought after thought or life after life, until they attain enlightenment and escape from the wheel of suffering. Suffering on this wheel is relative. Gods in heaven lead mostly blissful lives, while the sufferers in hell go from pain to pain. Demons and men experience more suffering than gods but less than hungry ghosts and beasts.

82. *True practice.* Practice that leads directly to enlightenment, as opposed to practice that leads to another stage of practice. Here true practice refers to beholding the mind.

83. *Ten good deeds*. These include the avoidance of the ten evil deeds, namely, murder, theft, adultery, falsehood, slander, profanity, gossip, avarice, anger, and advocating false views.

84. *Five precepts*. These are for lay Buddhists. They are injunctions against murder, theft, adultery, falsehood, and intoxication.

85. *Three asankhya kalpas*. A universe is marked by three phases: creation, duration, and destruction. Each lasts countless (*asankhya*) kalpas. A fourth phase of emptiness between universes isn't included here because it contains no hardships.

86. *Final age*. The first period of a buddha-age lasts 500 years, after which understanding of the correct doctrine begins to decline. The second period lasts 1,000 years, during which time understanding of the doctrine declines even further. The third and final period, the duration of which is indefinite, witnesses the eventual disappearance of a buddha's message. Another version assigns 500 years to each of the three periods.

87. *Three sets of precepts*. There are five for ordinary lay Buddhists, eight for the more devout members of the laity, and ten for novice monks and nuns. The first five are injunctions against murder, theft, adultery, falsehood, and intoxication. To these five are added injunctions against bodily adornment (garlands, jewelry, and perfume), bodily comfort (soft beds), and overeating (eating after the noon meal). And to these eight are added injunctions against the enjoyment of entertainment and the possession of wealth. These three sets are summarized by the three vows. The vow to avoid evil is made by all believers. The vow to cultivate virtue is made by the more devout lay believers. And the vow to liberate all beings is made by all monks and nuns.

88. *Paramitas . . . means to the other shore*. The six paramitas begin with charity and proceed through morality and patience, devotion and meditation to wisdom. Likening the paramitas to a boat that ferries people to the other shore, Buddhists see charity as the emptiness without which a boat can't float: morality as the keel, patience the hull, devotion the mast, meditation the sail, and wisdom the tiller.

89. *Milk . . . gruel*. After engaging in ascetic practices for a number of years to no avail, Shakyamuni broke his fast by drinking this milk-gruel offered by Nandabala, daughter of a cowherd chieftain. After drinking it, he sat down under a tree and resolved not to rise until he had attained enlightenment.

90. *Vairocana.* The Great Sun Buddha, who embodies the dharma-self or true body of the Buddha. As such, Vairocana is the central figure in the pantheon of five dhyani buddhas, which includes Akshobhya in the East, Ratnasambhava in the South, Amitabha in the West, and Amogasiddhi in the North.

91. *Six periods.* Morning, noon, afternoon, evening, midnight, and predawn.

92. *Stupas.* A stupa is a mound of earth or any structure erected over the remains, relics, or scriptures of a buddha. Walking around stupas is done in a clockwise direction, with the right shoulder always pointed toward the stupa.

93. *Five kinds of . . . incense.* These correspond to the five attributes of a tathagata's body.

94. *Dipamkara.* Shakyamuni met Dipamkara Buddha at the end of the second asankhya kalpa and offered him five blue lotuses Dipamkara then predicted Shakyamuni's future buddhahood. Thus Dipamkara appears whenever a buddha preaches the Dharma of the *Lotus Sutra.*

95. *Curl.* One of a buddha's thirty-two auspicious signs is a curl between his brows that emits rays of light.

96. *Six attractions.* That to which the six senses become attached.

97. *Lord.* A translation of *bhagavan*, one of a buddha's ten titles. The Chinese translation renders it *world-honored one.*

98. *Bathhouse Sutra.* Translated by An Shih-kao in the middle of the second century. This brief sutra recounts the merit gained from providing bathing facilities for monks.

99. *Inner garment.* One of the three regulation garments of a monk. The inner garment is worn to protect against desire. The seven-patch robe is worn to protect against anger. And the twenty-five-patch assembly robe is worn to protect against delusion.

100. *Western Paradise.* Also called the Pure Land. This land is presided over by Amitabha, one of the five dhyani buddhas and the one associated with the West. Wholehearted invocation of Amitabha assures the devotee of rebirth in his Pure Land, which is described as millions of miles away and not very far at all. Once reborn there, devotees have little trouble understanding the Dharma and attaining liberation.